THE PEOPLE WE WANTED TO FORGET

By

Michael G. Harpold

Book Publishers Network
CHANGING THE WORLD ONE BOOK AT A TIME

Book Publishers Network
P.O. Box 2256
Bothell • WA • 98041
Ph • 425-483-3040
www.bookpublishersnetwork.com

10 9 8 7 6 5 4 3 2 1
Printed in the United States of America

LCCN 2018939601
ISBN 978-1-945271-68-7

Cover art by Ketchikan, Alaska artist David Rubin

To the many who, without thought of personal consequence or expectation of acclaim, follow their conscience and do the right thing.

PROLOGUE

Sunday Morning, January 18, 1978, Songkhla, Thailand

THEIR EYES WIDE BUT UNSEEING as if they were prey gripped in the iron jaws of a predator, the refugees huddled in eerie silence on the open deck of their wooden fishing boat. Mothers and fathers, the men half-naked, clutched their children to their sides. They took no notice of our arrival. *They know they're going to die,* I realized. My heart stopped.

Tethered to the stern of a steel-hulled Thai navy gunboat, their small boat, once painted light blue with gay red trim, was so overcrowded I feared it would capsize the moment it left the dock. Twin .50-caliber machine guns mounted on the fantail of the naval vessel pointed menacingly down at the people. The throaty rumble of the ship's diesel engines signaled its impatience to get under way.

American vice consul Bob Hayashida and I ran to a Thai official dressed in casual shirt and slacks, standing at the foot of the gunboat's gangway, who appeared to be in charge.

"Can we talk to the people?" Hayashida asked.

"Yes," the official answered, recognizing Hayashida. "But in ten minutes we are towing them out to sea—beyond Thai waters."

"Can we talk to the vice governor?" Hayashida pressed.

"The vice governor is visiting in another province and cannot be contacted," the official replied.

Hayashida and I had been at breakfast on the lanai of my hotel that pleasant Sunday morning when a French doctor with Médecins Sans Frontièrs pushed his way through the shrubbery to the rail and told us the Thai navy was preparing to tow a boat loaded with refugees back out to sea.

"The people are in poor shape," the doctor said. "Many of the women have been raped, the men beaten. The children are sick from drinking seawater. I treated them as best as I could on the deck of their boat. I don't believe they can survive another night at sea, especially the children," the doctor added.

Praying that we would not be too late, we ran to Hayashida's car and raced to the dock. It appeared that the vice governor of Songkhla was about to make good on the threat he had delivered at a reception the previous afternoon to visiting Deputy Assistant Secretary of State for East Asia and Pacific Affairs Robert Oakley, and more Vietnamese boat people were about to die.

Ambassador Oakley had flown to Songkhla to try to persuade the governor to treat refugees more humanely. I was in Thailand to gather facts about the Vietnamese boat people for a congressional hearing and had been given a seat on the embassy aircraft. When we had arrived the previous afternoon, Oakley had insisted that I attend the official reception where he somewhat grandly, I thought, introduced me as the special assistant to the commissioner of the Immigration and Naturalization Service.

At the reception, the vice governor would have nothing of Oakley's plea for restraint. After relating the long history of the United States ignoring Thai pleas to take Vietnamese refugees off their hands, he proclaimed that he would continue to force refugee boats back out to sea until the United States started taking the Vietnamese from the overcrowded camp in Songkhla and resettled them elsewhere in the free world. Oakley had been unable to commit the United States to take in the refugees and earlier that morning had flown back to Bangkok.

Hayashida and I hurried back to the refugee boat.

"Who is the captain?" I asked, my Vietnamese grown rusty in the decade since I served in Vietnam. After some hesitation, a half-dozen men rose to their feet and identified themselves as the committee who made decisions for the group.

"How many are you?" I asked.

"We are thirteen men, five women, and sixteen children from Phuc Quoc Island," a spokesman said. "We are three families." One of the men retrieved a map, a page torn from a schoolbook, showing in four colors the countries along the rim of the Western Pacific, and pointed to a dot off the southern tip of South Vietnam.

"We want to go to Australia," the spokesman said.

I shot Hayashida a puzzled look.

"They know the United States won't take them," the vice consul said and looked away.

I winced but pressed on.

"Is this all you have to navigate?" I asked, astounded that they would set sail on a 2,500-mile voyage having only a map torn from an elementary school textbook. From the wheelhouse, the men produced a compass mounted on a block of wood that had apparently been salvaged from the instrument panel of a wrecked aircraft.

"What will you do for food and water," I asked.

"Nobody eats much because we are mostly sick from drinking sea water," the spokesman said, and I dropped the issue.

The men related that they had set sail as part of a larger group of 180 from their village. On their first night at sea, they had become separated from the other boats. They had been at sea three days, they said. During the night, their motor had failed, and they had drifted into Songkhla.

"First, Thai pirates, and then even Thai fishermen, overtook our boat four times," the men said. "They take everything we have: three watches, two rings, and two necklaces." The spokesman showed me the welts where his watch was ripped from his wrist. The refugees managed to retain a single US twenty-dollar bill that one of the men had concealed in his rectum.

I asked about the herringbone-like rows of welts on the backs of several men.

"We are fishermen and the Communists made us give them our entire catch," a man said. "They would not give us back enough food to feed our families. We are starving. We tried to flee before, but we were caught and beaten."

"Where are your clothes?" I asked, gesturing to men clad only in underpants.

"Each time the Thais boarded us, they beat up the men and raped the women and girls, right in front of their children and husbands. They threatened to throw anyone who resisted into the ocean. Then they took the women's clothing to shame them. Afterwards, the men gave up their clothing to the women."

I looked at Hayashida; his grimace acknowledged our helplessness.

"We should take down their names," he suggested. "Sometime, somewhere, someone may want to know what happened to them." He retrieved a yellow legal pad from his car, and we began a task that I could equate only to a census of the doomed.

Our allotted time ticking away, my mind desperately churned for options. If the Thai gunboat started to leave the dock with the refugee boat in tow, I was certain I'd be forced to jump aboard the little fishing boat and be towed out to sea with them. Would the Thai sailors forcibly remove me, leaving my gambit for naught? If I succeeded in going out to sea with the refugees, and if a rescue failed to materialize or the small boat floundered, I could lose my life and have accomplished nothing.

But failing to act would leave me to face a lifetime of horror and self-doubt that I knew I would not be able to bear.

Or I could lie, try to convince the governor I had the authority to guarantee that the refugees would be taken to the United States. If I could get them into the camp, I'd have a chance to persuade my superiors in the State Department and the Justice Department to accept them as political refugees.

But would the vice governor believe me, or was this just wishful thinking? Ambassador Oakley had told him the previous day that the boat people were merely fleeing bad economic conditions, not political repression, and therefore were not eligible to be taken in by the United States. Any promise I made, valid or not, would not only contravene what Oakley had said but also underscore the shallowness of the US policy.

It occurred to me that I might be playing directly into the vice governor's hand, but so be it, I thought. It appeared to be the only chance the people huddled on the boat had. There would be consequences for me. I was certain to lose my job and possibly would face criminal prosecution for misrepresenting my authority in an official matter, but there was no comparing a setback to my career with the loss of thirty-four innocent lives.

The pitch of the gunboats engines dropped. Sailors took their posts at the lines. The Thai official started towards Hayashida and me, signaling that our time was up.

1

Saigon, South Vietnam, Sunday, September 10, 1968

THE NOONDAY SUN HAD CAST NO SHADOW, and the atmosphere itself was so steamy it seemed to glow as we drove into the heart of Saigon in Murray's small, black sedan. The car did not have air conditioning. Murray, a fit, middle-age man with close-cropped, blond hair wore slacks and a casual shirt. I shed my necktie. Less than an hour after I had stepped from the cool interior of a sleek Cathay Pacific DC-8, I wanted a shower.

Trapped in a mélange of exotic vehicles, we whirred along a tree-lined avenue as if in a cloud of locusts. Intense Vietnamese men on Honda motorbikes rode so close to the side of our car I could have easily reached out and touched them. Trim women in flowery *ao dais* and high heels perched sidesaddle behind their husbands while three or even four tiny children straddled the metal carrier tightly nested behind their mother.

Dignified Vietnamese men in dark suits, their ladies perfectly coiffed and made-up despite the hot, sticky atmosphere, rode in long-hooded, black Citroëns. Muscular, bronzed men in shorts, sandals, and conical straw hats strained at the pedals of black-hooded trishaws. Their colorfully enameled, motorized, three-wheel cousins spewed oily exhaust from noisy two-cylinder engines. Diminutive yellow and blue Renault taxis impatiently beeped their horns. The horde paused at a traffic light.

"See how the light is placed on the near side of the intersection instead of on the far side like in the US," Murray, pointed out. "That's to keep people from blocking cross traffic when they stop for a red light. That's the way it had to be in the US fifty years ago when automobiles first started to come into popular use."

I nodded, wondering where Murray was going with the point.

Saigon soccer mom.

"That's the way a lot of things are here, including the government," he said. "Change must wait for the people, and the Vietnamese are behind, in some things centuries behind, and trying to catch up. All the while, they're trying to fight a war."

Recently hired by the United States Agency for International Development, USAID, I had felt in ways that I was behind, too. I was just thirty, and in a further twist, I was slated to be the first US advisor to be embedded with the paramilitary National Police Field Force who was not a former Green Beret. The retired Special Forces officers and NCOs, like Murray, who worked with the NPFF had had years of training and combat experience in Vietnam. I had none. I sensed Murray evaluating me.

We were moving again, and olive-drab military trucks roared, disgorging diesel fumes. Green-uniformed Vietnamese soldiers crowded in the beds of the trucks gawked down at us. At major intersections, Vietnamese police and soldiers peered at the cavalcade from behind barbed wire and green-sandbag barricades.

"Why am I not seeing any American soldiers?" I asked Murray.

"Saigon is off limits to most GIs because they're easy targets for terrorists," Murray said. "Also, we don't want to be viewed as an occupier, so most Americans are out in the boonies or on big logistics bases like Long Binh. Both countries want to keep the US presence in Saigon low-key."

We drove past the gleaming-white Presidential Palace set behind a high, iron fence, the tennis courts and polo field at Le Circle Sportif, and the large, fortress-like American embassy before turning onto Nguyễn Huệ Street. A classic French boulevard, the thoroughfare was separated from the curb lanes by narrow, curbed islands harboring tall, chestnut trees girdled with black, iron staves and crowded with colorful kiosks.

Murray pulled up in front of a small, street-front hotel, the Hôtel Oscar. To prevent casualties from flying glass in the event of a bomb blast, the windows of the Oscar had been replaced by opaque, plastic sheeting.

Perched on a tall stool behind a high counter, a bald-headed European presided over the small lobby furnished with worn leather chairs and potted ferns. A red and green parrot in a cage cackled incessantly. An open-latticed, French elevator wheezed and rattled to the upper seven floors of the hotel.

As I finished registering, four men in khaki uniforms, their epaulets and shoulder patches identifying them as Canadian, Polish, and Indian army officers, exited the lobby. Out on the street, they piled into two Land Rovers displaying white flags with the insignia of the International Control Commission. I looked at Murray quizzically.

"They're here to report violations of the Geneva Peace Accords that partitioned the country fourteen years ago," Murray explained.

"What do they say about the North Vietnamese Army camped out in the jungle twenty miles from here?" I asked.

"Nothing. No Communist violations of the accords are ever reported," Murray said. "All members of the team have to agree on what they see. The Communist-bloc Polish members, and sometimes even the Indians—they get their arms from the Russians, veto the reports of the Canadians."

"And that brings us to why we're here, right?" I said.

"Yep. South Vietnam is where Eisenhower and Kennedy drew the line," Murray said.

The Oscar was not plush, not like the Caravelle on the next block over that housed the world press corps, but it did offer air conditioning—noisy window units that expelled a stream of dank, humid air, eclipsing the efforts of an ancient ceiling fan that whirred uselessly overhead. In a tiled corner above a floor drain, a showerhead protruded from the wall. A plastic curtain hanging from a quarter-circle track protected the remainder of the room from the spray. Geckos clung motionless to the damp plaster walls and ceiling. I resisted the urge to prod one to see if it was alive.

That evening, Murray returned, and we walked down Nguyễn Huệ Street to the Club Américain, the name scripted in red neon above the entrance. I was stopped at the door for lack of a tie.

"Use your belt," Murray commanded, and after complying, I was let into the darkened interior.

On the stage at the far end of the room, an Asian Connie Francis belted out "Where the Boys Are," accompanied by a small band that didn't quite have the beat. The clientele were a mix of American and Vietnamese men, some in military uniforms. At small tables, middle-aged men in white short-sleeve shirts and ties sat across from gaudily costumed and garishly made-up Vietnamese hostesses.

A tall, skinny American sporting a black Stetson, leather vest, and chaps sauntered John Wayne style up to the bar. Slung low on his hips was a brace of .44-caliber revolvers. I noted the guns were loaded and looked quizzically at Murray. He shrugged.

"There're a lot of civilians over here who work for big US contractors, Kellogg, Brown and Root, even Foremost Dairies," Murray explained. "Then there're guys like that, adventurers and others acting out their fantasies."

We ordered drinks, "33," a local beer that came in a large, brown bottle. It was suitably cold.

"A lot of guys employed by the news agencies, USAID, diplomats, business people, government officials of all types come here, all looking to make contacts," Murray explained. "It's also a place you can bring your Vietnamese counterpart when he wants to have a little fun.

"Madame Nhu, the Dragon Lady, is supposed to have owned this place before her brother-in-law, President Diệm, and her husband, Ngô Đình Nhu, were assassinated and she fled to Paris. Nhu was minister of interior and head of the National Police. She's the one who called immolations of monks "Buddhist barbeques." There's still a lot of intrigue. The Special Branch police hang out here and their CIA counterparts."

"Is this where Fowler meets Gigot of the French *sureté*?" I quipped. "How about Alden Pyle, is this where he plots with the rebel commander?"

"I don't know," Murray said. "But it's a safe bet Graham Greene had a drink or two here," he added, picking up on the reference to characters in the novel, *The Quiet American*.

We ordered steaks. Fresh out of Vietnamese language classes, on my first night in Vietnam, it was not the sort of evening I had anticipated—I had been given the address of a Vietnamese café by one of my language tutors—but the food was good enough.

Back at the Oscar, I climbed the stairs to the rooftop and savored the cool night breeze. Orange parachute flares popped and drifted down over the nearby Saigon River, infamous for pirates and now the Viet Cong, who hid among Vietnamese peasants and fishermen who lived on the junks and sampans rafted along the riverbank and in the harbor.

I listened to the muffled whump of exploding artillery shells in the distance. In Greene's day, it was the Communist Viet Minh who hid in that darkened jungle. Now it was the North Vietnamese Army who threatened the city. On my first night in Saigon, it all felt very romantic.

In my thoughts, I drifted back to Greene's character, Alden Pyle, a young civil servant abroad, idealistic, naïve, believing his country could bring peace and stability to an Asian nation at war with itself and create a stable, democratic bulwark against the pernicious advance of Communism. Now, my generation was deployed against the Communists, so near I could hear the guns, and I was that young, civil servant abroad, eager to get out into the countryside and be part of the war.

Graham Greene's story ended tragically for Pyle. *How will it end for me? How will it end for the South Vietnamese?*

2

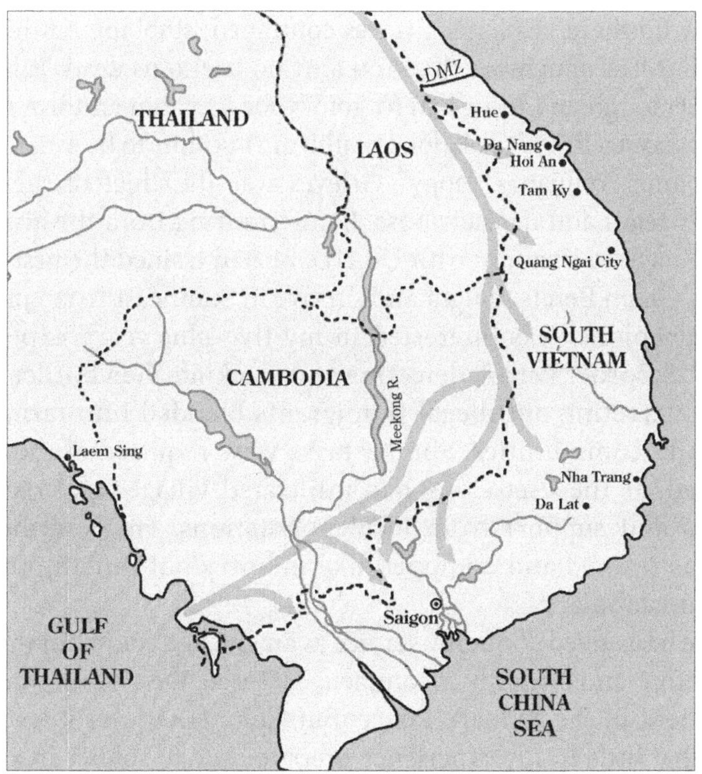

Republic of South Vietnam

"I'M SENDING YOU UP TO TAM KY," Colonel Grieves announced. "You're going to be on your own up there." The quiet, greying man with heavy jowls and droopy eyelids and dressed in a Hawaiian shirt and grey slacks took a long draw on his cigarette. I had only the vaguest idea where Tam Ky was but sensed it was a province or district town in the northern part of the country.

We sat across from each other on flimsy metal chairs drinking Cokes at a shaded table on the patio at the National Police Field Force advisor's compound. The concrete walls and the red tile roof of the warehouse that served as his headquarters still bore gaping holes and pockmarks inflicted by exploding shells and bullets during the Communist assault on the Chợ Lớn district of Saigon during Tet, eight months earlier.

"Son, I ain't got the time to teach you everything you're gonna need to know up there," Colonel Grieves continued, stubbing out his cigarette. "But just remember this. You ain't no use to us dead. When the goin' gets tough and things aren't goin' your way, run and live to fight another day. Hell! We've all done that! It ain't nothin' to be ashamed of."

Colonel William "Pappy" Grieves was the chief of the NPFF advisory team and my new boss. Before retiring from the army and coming back to Vietnam with USAID, he had trained the first generation of Green Berets to fight and survive in Southeast Asian jungles.[1]

The colonel was interested in my five-plus years' experience in the US Border Patrol, detecting and tracking alien border crossers and ferreting out illegal immigrants blended into farm labor crews and communities. Similar tasks were required of the NPFF, he noted, as the Viet Cong had infiltrated villages and recruited fighters and support from local populations. He described the NPFF as trained and equipped like infantry but functioning as a rural constabulary.

We had talked about my service as an enlisted soldier in the army both before and after my incomplete career at West Point, the latter assignment in the Military Police. But Colonel Grieves knew, and I knew, that little in my experience prepared me to soldier in a counterinsurgency campaign in the Vietnamese jungle. Still, he had chosen me for this assignment, and I trusted him to not send me into a situation he knew I couldn't handle. We finished our Cokes in silence.

1. In the Ngo Dinh Diem regime under Madame Nhu and her brother, the NPFF had been the brutal enforcers of a corrupt and insensitive government. Now, under President Thieu, Colonel Grieves had been given a free hand to transform the NPFF into a well-functioning constabulary and become the primary reaction force of the counterinsurgency campaign. Grieves kicked out the often rogue band of Australian mercenaries, who under a CIA contract had previously advised the police, and recruited a team of retired US Special Forces officers and NCOs to train the NPFF.

"Good luck!" Colonel Grieves said as we rose from the table and shook hands.

Earlier in the afternoon, my host, Murray, had outfitted me with field gear: a flak jacket and a steel helmet, several sets of the largest available size of the brown-camouflage uniform of the NPFF, and jungle boots. He handed me a World War II vintage M2 carbine—a weapon far inferior to the VC's AK-47s—and a police model .38-caliber revolver. I was familiar with both, but I was surprised to find them still in use.

"Until we can get M16s, it's what the NPFF are armed with, and you'll have to depend on them for ammo," Murray explained. Handing me a large, brown bottle of a new anti-bacterial drug, tetracycline, he said, "Use these for just about everything." Then he asked, "Have you been given malaria pills, yet?"

"I started taking them at the Foreign Service Institute," I replied.

"Take these along with your regular pills," Murray instructed, passing me a bottle of large, white tablets. "They give you a bellyache, but they prevent cerebral malaria, and boy, you don't want to get that."

That night on the rooftop of the Hôtel Oscar, I thought a lot about my wife, Dominica, and our three daughters at home in Bakersfield, California, who were too young to understand where their daddy had gone or why. My talk with Colonel Grieves had been sobering. *What if* . . . I asked myself for a moment. *What would it be like for them to grow up without their father?*

A half-million American men, my generation, were out in that dark jungle, dropping the illumination flares and firing the artillery rounds I could see and hear from the rooftop of the Oscar. Like me, many were fathers. Many of them had not volunteered. Nonetheless, we served. It was our duty. Even though I had already completed a stateside enlistment in the army, I believed I should be out there, too.

We had come of age in the shadow of WWII. Our parents, our uncles and aunts, were veterans of that war, and we understood that one day we, too, would serve our country. We already filled the ranks of the large, peacetime army, preparing to defend Europe against further Soviet invasion. The threat was real. In the post-colonial world, the Soviets aggressively promoted wars of national liberation, training and encouraging local Communists and supplying them with the arms to conduct guerilla warfare against shaky governments in newly emerging, post-WWII nations.

In 1959, Cuba fell to Communist revolutionary Fidel Castro. Three years later, the Soviet Union deployed nuclear-tipped missiles on the island ninety miles from the United States. Most frightening of all were the Soviet Union's nuclear weapons, and it had the means to deliver them to American cities. Towns, businesses, even families built bomb shelters and debated if it was ethical to shoot your neighbor if he was trying to get into yours. At school, kids practiced "duck and cover" in the event of a Soviet nuclear attack. My generation grew up worrying about our future, even the future of civilization, yet we carried on with our lives and dreams.

Military service was required of all physically fit young men, and approaching the end of high school, we decided whether we would enlist then or seek a deferment in order to complete college. But we all served, before college or after, married or unmarried, father with young children or not, and we understood the necessity for it. It was our duty, and my sense of it had brought me to Vietnam.

I was one of the many boys who, growing up in our small, rural Wisconsin town during WWII, stood on the curb waving a hand-colored, paper American flag as convoys of olive-drab trucks loaded with soldiers passed through on the highway to and from nearby Camp McCoy. Enthralled by the stories related by returning veterans, my imagination had been caught up by the careers of legendary WWII heroes such as Eisenhower, MacArthur, Patton, and Bradley, all graduates of the US Military Academy at West Point, and I dreamed that one day I would follow in their footsteps. But as the end of high school approached, I was painfully aware that my grades were not good enough to attract a congressional appointment.

When I turned seventeen, I joined our local Army Reserve unit and spent the entire summer between my junior and senior years of high school on active duty for training. I enrolled in a correspondence course for officers. In the course materials, I learned that competitive appointments to West Point were available to twenty-five enlisted men each year. Candidates were not required to have completed high school. I saw my chance, skipped high school graduation, and enlisted in the Regular Army.

After completing basic and branch training, in the fall, I was sent to the US Military Academy Preparatory School run by the Army for enlisted applicants at Stewart AFB, New York, near West Point. The courses in math and English and the physical training were just what I needed, and the next spring, after competing on the physical agility test and the Scholastic Aptitude Test and passing the medical exam, I learned I had won one of the coveted army appointments.

Two months later, on a hot, early July evening, standing bareheaded on Trophy Point dressed in our new, grey wool uniforms, right hands raised, I and 731 other new cadets of the USMA Class of 1961 took the Oath of Allegiance. The band played "On Wisconsin" and "Men of Wisconsin." I allowed myself to believe that the marches had been played just for me. It was the proudest moment of my life.

My stars seemed aligned for a career in the army, but my life soon took a zag. I had dated Dominica for over a year and fallen deeply in love with her. She lived near West Point and visited nearly every weekend. Our relationship strengthened as I supported her through a long recuperation following a car accident that nearly cost her life. In the fall of my yearling, or second year, at the academy, we discovered we were soon to be parents. I had adopted the West Point motto, "Duty, Honor, Country," as the ideal that would guide my life. To it, I now appended "Family."

Cadets were not permitted to marry, and concerned for the future of our child, I decided to leave the academy. I was sent to Ft. Bliss, Texas, to finish my enlistment. Our daughter, Dominica, was born in May.

After my discharge in February 1960, I went to work for a finance company in El Paso. That fall, Dominica received a settlement from the auto accident, and we decided to use it for me to go back to school. We moved to Madison, Wisconsin, and I enrolled in the university, choosing to study civil engineering. Our second daughter, Michelle, was born in March. A year later, Kathryn was born.

But I did not do well in engineering. After two semesters and summer school, the dean suggested I try another major, and I switched to the humanities. Meanwhile, our money was running low. I had applied for a federal civil service job, just in case, and in the fall of 1962, in the middle of the Cuban Missile Crisis, I got a call from the US Border Patrol. The patrol was beefing up its force on the Gulf Coast and the Mexican border. Could I report for duty at Calexico, California, in two weeks? I had never looked back on my decision to leave West Point, but I felt my service to country was as yet incomplete. I reported for duty as requested.

I liked duty in the border patrol, spending long nights in the deserts east and west of Calexico. Because I worked mostly at night, I enrolled in Imperial Valley College. In 1965, I was transferred to the newly opened station in Bakersfield and was able to complete my degree at the local campus of Fresno State University.

Meanwhile, in Southeast Asia, the British were fighting Communist guerillas in Malaya. Across the Gulf of Thailand in Indochina, the Viet Minh insurgents led by Communist Ho Chi Minh had defeated the French. The country was partitioned, but there was no peace as the Communist north continued to subvert and infiltrate the south. Then, in Laos, the government fell to a coalition led by Communists. President Kennedy decided the United States would make a stand in South Vietnam.

Our big brothers and sisters fought in Korea, and now it was our turn in Vietnam. My West Point classmates were already completing their first combat tours. I yearned to be there, too. Now with a college degree and five-plus years of service in the border patrol, I applied for an officer's commission in the Military Police Corps, but a Pentagon general decided I didn't deserve a second chance.

Undeterred, I answered an ad in the *Los Angeles Times* for men and women with law enforcement backgrounds to go to Vietnam for two years and help train and advise the Vietnamese National Police.

3

THE SILVER, 1940S VINTAGE, TWIN-ENGINE DC-3, waiting to board passengers on the tarmac at Tan Son Nhut, was straight out of that era's Milton Caniff comic strip, *Terry and the Pirates*, but this one was owned by Air America, a company created by the CIA to support US civil operations in Southeast Asia. The fabric-covered airliner seats were worn, and the backlit seatbelt and no smoking signs displayed only Chinese characters. But instead of Hot Shot Charlie and the Dragon Lady, the pilots were American and wore white shirts with blue epaulets, blue trousers, and billed caps typical of commercial airline pilots.

I was on my way to Dalat, the site of the National Police Field Force training school. The city was most notably a resort for wealthy and powerful Saigonese who found the cool mountain air and pine forests in the central highlands a welcome change from the heat and intrigues of the South Vietnamese capital. To my surprise, my former roommate from USAID orientation days in Washington, DC, Bill Jackson, met me at the airport. Bill was a retired Special Forces lieutenant colonel and had gone to Vietnam ahead of me while I remained at the Foreign Service Institute for language training.

In Arlington, Bill had been especially fond of chicken gizzards, necks, feet, and limp greens, food I jokingly called his Green Beret cuisine. Often upon returning to our apartment in the late afternoon, I would find our door propped open, the hallway filled with smoke, and Bill frying a pan of chicken parts on the stove in our tiny kitchen. I wondered what I would have to eat during my stay at his house.

Bill shared the house with Chuck Petrie and Morris Looney, also retired Special Forces officers assigned to the NPFF training facility. They put me up in a spare bedroom, but the week did not start well.

Sunday was rainy and cool, and in the afternoon, we sat around talking and drinking beer. We were preparing to grill some steaks when an excited Vietnamese man pounded on the door. A gunfight had broken out at the training center between the NPFF trainees and the Nung hired to provide security at the training center. We piled into a Jeep and rushed up the mountain to the NPFF barracks.

"The Nung are ethnic Chinese who've lived for centuries in Vietnam and still speak their native language," Bill explained. "The South Vietnamese government doesn't trust them and won't let them serve in the army, but the Special Forces hires a lot of them. They've proven to be good fighters and intensely loyal. That's why we hire them at the training center, too."

"The only problem is that the Vietnamese and the Nung hate each other," Chuck added, "and that leads to scraps between them and the trainees."

When we arrived at the NPFF barracks, we found the trainees armed, agitated, and in disarray. No one seemed to be in charge, and it took a while to sort out. It emerged that earlier that afternoon, a group of armed Nung had commandeered a loaded civilian bus. Riding on top, they hosed down the NPFF barracks with automatic weapon fire as they passed the facility on their way down the mountain. In Dalat, they commandeered another bus and fired again at the barracks as they passed on the way back up to their camp. This time, the NPFF trainees fired back. Chuck, Bill, and Morris conferred and decided they would go to the Nung camp and try to calm things down.

"You stay here and keep yourself visible," Chuck instructed, thrusting a WWII vintage M1 rifle into my hands. "The Nung won't fire on the trainees if an American is present." I stationed myself conspicuously in a second floor window opening where I was sure to be spotted from the road.

I'm supposed to convince two hundred panicked trainees to trust that I can protect them if the Nung come back? What the hell do I do if they show up? Do I shoot first or wait to get shot at? How do I stop the Vietnamese from shooting at the Nung? Mine was a small assignment in the scheme of things, but I could also sense that I was being tested. I was the first NPFF advisor hired without Special Forces experience. Colonel Grieves had put his trust in me, and I was now on the spot.

After what seemed a very long hour, Bill, Chuck, and Morris returned, confident they had quieted the Nung and the danger was past. I had not spotted any Nung in the interim, and I was quite relieved.

I was scheduled to fly back to Saigon on Air America Saturday morning and, the following day, catch an Air America flight to Danang, en route to Tam Ky, but when Bill and I arrived at the airport, I learned I had been bumped.

"The CIA owns Air America, and their employees have first priority on seating," Bill explained. He pointed out a second aircraft refueling on the tarmac, a twin-engine C-123 transport plane in green and black camouflage paint. The plane had no markings, only the initials "Cas" stenciled in small black letters on the nose.

"Why don't you see if you can get a hop with them?" Bill suggested. "Continental Air Services—Cas, 'the company'—has been the cover for CIA operations in Southeast Asia since World War II," he explained. "Over here, you learn to grab the first aircraft available. Give it a try; there might not be another aircraft arriving here today."

Unmarked C-123 flew author from Dalat to Saigon with a stop in the jungle somewhere in Southeast Asia.

Three Asian crewmen neatly dressed in civilian, dark-blue trousers, white shirts with blue and silver epaulets, and blue airline-pilot caps waited under the wing for the plane to finish fueling. Their round faces and stocky build appeared more typically Chinese than Vietnamese, I thought. Nevertheless, I tried my new language skills, lifting my voice an octave to accommodate the tones that were essential to spoken Vietnamese.

"Đại úy làm ơn chở tôi đến Sài Gòn?" I asked.

The three crewmen looked at me blankly. I repeated my request in English but got the same result.

"Here, let me show you how it's done," Bill said brushing past me. Linking his thumbs and imitating the wings of an aircraft in flight with his fingers, then pointing to his chest, he said to the captain, "You gimmee go-go Shai-gon?"

Grinning, the three crewmen vigorously nodded their heads yes. When the pilot signaled the aircraft was ready to go, I waved goodbye to Bill, grabbed my gear, and hopped up the rear loading ramp into the cargo bay. Following the crew chief's gestures, I edged past three strapped-down pallets of bagged cement and pulled down a web seat next to a porthole.

But the plane didn't go directly to Saigon. About an hour out of Dalat, we began to circle low over triple-canopy jungle. Peering through a porthole, I spotted a long, deep slash cut through into dark-green jungle. The reddish-clay soil gave it the appearance of an open wound. But I couldn't see any sign of a town, not even the thatch houses of a hamlet. As we landed, I noted the runway was surfaced with PCV, perforated metal grating used for temporary airstrips during WWII. Curiously, no buildings stood alongside the landing strip, only green jungle.

Seemingly at no particular point, we taxied off the edge of the PCV, but no one was there to greet us. It was midday, hot, and I followed the aircrew to the shade at the base of a tree. Presently, an ancient Chevrolet stake-bed truck emerged from the jungle, accompanied by a crew of men wearing black pajamas and conical straw hats. I watched drowsily as the men passed the cement, bag by bag, from the cargo bay and stacked it on the bed of the truck.

I was startled to consciousness by a muffled thonk from the jungle behind us—a distinct, hollow explosion I immediately recognized as a mortar shell leaving a tube. A hundred yards down the runway, a plume of red dirt and smoke spewed into the air followed by a blast. The aircrew leapt to their feet and raced to their airplane. I scrambled after them. The captain hastily climbed to the cockpit and kicked the engines to life. Clambering into the cargo bay, I joined the second officer and the crew chief shoving and kicking at the half-unloaded and now unrestrained pallets of cement.

The engines roared in our ears drowning out the shouts of the natives and the pilots. Outside the aircraft, another explosion spurred us on as we heaved loose bags of concrete and shoved half-unloaded pallets off the ramp as we rolled onto the runway. It seemed like forever, but the ramp started to lift and we were airborne. I grappled my way into my jump seat, bracing myself with my feet while I fought to buckle my harness. I was shaking, drenched with sweat, my head and heart pounding. Like a giant clamshell, the ramp finally closed. The aircraft climbed steeply and banked into a turn.

It was dark when we set down at Tan Son Nhut. Setting foot on the tarmac, the pilots, the crew chief, and I paused beside the aircraft before moving off on our separate ways. I wanted for all the world to ask where we had been that day, to reminisce about our close call, even to blurt, "Goddamn!" but language couldn't serve us. Instead, we shook hands over and over, bowed, and clapped each other on the back. I was happy to be alive. No wages for stevedoring were due.

Back at the Oscar, I went one last time to the rooftop. The Saigon air that evening felt very good. I had learned that beyond satisfying an internal need to serve my country, beyond helping the Vietnamese, staying alive was first above all else.

In the morning, I'd be on my way to another unknown—Tam Ky.

4

Mimicking the Vietnamese police officers arrayed around the cooking fire, I squatted back on the heels of my jungle boots drawing the fabric of my new, brown cammies so tight that I feared my knees would bust through the fabric. My hip and thigh muscles burned, and my legs were numb from the unaccustomed position. It seemed as if an hour had passed, but it had been only minutes. Giving up, steadying myself, with one hand, I rolled back onto the balls of my feet, dreading the moment I would be obliged to stand.

The low flames of the fire cast an orange glow on the brick walls of the darkened barracks where Major Anh, two companies of his National Police Field Force battalion, and I waited in the yard to depart at midnight for the pre-dawn mission. Policemen lounged on their gear, slept, or talked in low voices. Some of the men played cards or dice. Constrained by the limits of my still-embryonic Vietnamese vocabulary, Major Ahn and I struggled to extend our conversation beyond introductions.

Major Anh's wife, Bå Anh, roasted thin strips of meat tied into split bamboo sticks over the hot embers of the fire. When they were ready, the slender woman dressed in black silk pajamas and a drab, grey blouse, passed them one by one to her husband and the other officers squatting around the fire. At her husband's prompt, she passed a stick to me. Following my host's lead, I chewed at the exposed edges, working the tangy morsels from the split bamboo with my tongue. When I finished, I followed Major Anh's lead and tossed the stick into the fire. Bå Anh promptly passed me another.

"Cái nây là gì?" I asked Major Anh when I had finished, curious about the meat I had just consumed.

"*Thịt chó*," he replied.

I didn't understand and looked at him quizzically.

"Thịt chó," he repeated with emphasis.

Still puzzled, I shook my head. Major Anh looked around the courtyard. *"Lá gí!"* he exclaimed brightly, jabbing his finger at a canine lounging at the outer edge of the firelight.

I nodded to show that I understood, but I was caught by surprise and struggled to keep my composure. That I was eating dog meat seemed so improbable I could not entirely believe it. I told myself that I had simply misunderstood, but my host had clearly pointed at a dog. When Bå Anh offered another stick, I smiled and shook my head no.

I could feel the chewed bits of dog meat congealing into a lump in my esophagus, but for the moment at least, the taboo flesh stayed down. I dreaded when it would come up: in front of my hosts, as we marched into the hamlet in the morning, in the middle of a firefight with the Viet Cong? Already nervous about this my first operation with the paramilitary police and going solo at that, I hovered on the verge of panic.

I had arrived in Danang late that afternoon after a long flight from Saigon in a silver Air America C-46, a WWII relic that looked like a shiny minnow out of water. Art Garza, the NPFF advisor assigned to Region 1 headquarters, met me on the tarmac. Like Colonel Grieves and the advisers at the training center in Dalat, Garza was a retired Green Beret officer. I expected to spend a couple of days with him before flying down to my first assignment in Tam Ky, but he had other ideas for me. The Marines had requested an NPFF unit for a cordon and search operation that night, and Garza thought it would be a good experience for me to go along.

The Viet Cong had been firing at aircraft taking off and landing at the Danang Air Base, and the Marines, who were responsible for the security of the base, had pinpointed a hamlet near the end of runway as the source of the fire. Under cover of darkness, the Marines planned to cordon off the hamlet to prevent escape, while at dawn the police would move through the cluster of thatch houses and search out the VC gun crew and their weapon. I suppressed panic when

Garza off-handedly mentioned he was not going along and I would be accompanying the police by myself.

Shortly before midnight, a convoy of trucks arrived accompanied by a US Marine lieutenant and a radioman. We loaded up and rode in darkness, the trucks relying on their small, guide lights. We traveled for about a half-hour and then dismounted and marched along the road in two columns. There was no moon, and I struggled to keep the faint outline of the policeman in front of me in view, at times clumsily reaching out and grasping his web gear.

Finally, we arrived at a bridge, but in the dark, it was impossible to gauge the size of the structure or the width of the river it spanned. The surface was paved—asphalt or aged concrete, I couldn't tell—but I could make out iron girders above us faintly outlined against the dark sky. I followed Major Anh and the two Marines past the shapes of reclining policemen and found a place to settle against the iron railing.

According to the plan, the Marines were to make their way along the far bank of the river to the hamlet, passing by our position on the bridge in the dark. Speaking in a low voice, the radio operator confirmed to the approaching Marine column that we were in position on the bridge.

The tropical night was pleasant and still, and I began to relax a little. Backlit by the ambient light of the nearby airbase, the tops of heavily leafed trees formed a dark horizon above the opposite riverbank. The lieutenant was from La Jolla, California, and in low voices, we talked about home. I asked about what he and his men thought about the war.

"It's our job, and as Marines we expect to do it," the lieutenant explained. "We know that back home some people are protesting the war, but we're proud to be Marines and doing what our country asks of us."

The thunderous roar of a lone jet aircraft taking off from the airbase rent the quiet night air and disrupted our conversation. The lieutenant said it was an F4 Phantom fighter-bomber, and I marveled at the aircraft's raw power. In silence, we watched the white-hot exhaust, like two inverted candles, rise into the black sky. Climbing rapidly, the flames turned to cauldron-like disks as the aircraft turned away from us.

Suddenly, from the direction of the hamlet, green tracer bullets arced upward in the Phantom's wake. As we watched, the emerald points of lights slowed, burned out, and fell away, far short of their speeding target. Raising his compass to his eye, the lieutenant noted the azimuth to the source of the bullets and called it in on his radio.

"Those are .51-caliber rounds fired from a Chinese-made machine gun," the lieutenant explained. "The Communists use green tracers, but you can't always count on that. They use a lot of the ammo they capture from us, too, and our tracers are red."

The visual proof that the Viet Cong was present in the hamlet both exhilarated and sobered me. Our conversation dying, I dozed.

We had been in place about an hour when suddenly the bridge was lit up amid a clamorous din. Red tracer rounds skipped off the asphalt deck in long red streaks. Bullets ricocheted off the iron railings and girders above our heads with frightening clangs. Bright showers of sparks spewed down on us as we cowered below. In the eerie light, I could see the taut faces of my companions.

I rolled from my sitting position, pressing myself as flat as I could on the deck, struggling to get my carbine to my shoulder, trying to grasp what was happening. Bullets cracked sharply as they whizzed past me. Answering the staccato blasts of automatic rifle fire from the dark riverbank, the police fired back at the rapidly blinking points of light. The crack of their carbines added to the din.

"Cease firing! Cease firing!" the lieutenant screamed into the radio. "Those are Marines!" he yelled to the Vietnamese policemen who could not understand him but caught the urgency of his alarm.

Major Anh shouted to his men. The fire from the jungle quieted, and the clamor on the bridge stopped. Officers moved among the men checking for casualties. Unbelievably, no one had been hurt.

In the darkness, the lead Marine rifle platoon edging its way along the riverbank had stumbled into the Vietnamese Popular Forces outpost guarding the bridge. Mistakenly believing they had walked into an ambush, the Marines opened fire with their M16s and M60 machine guns.

The Marine column continued its approach along the riverbank to the hamlet, but it was apparent that the element of surprise had now been lost. Nonetheless, the operation would proceed, and I settled back against the bridge railing and tried again to get some rest.

At first light, the police were on their feet. In a single column, we marched along a dirt path to the village a half-mile away. As we approached, I was startled by a loud pop and a whoosh from behind me. I took two running steps and flung myself on the ground. When I looked up, Major Anh was standing above me, grinning. He offered me his hand.

"Hand-flare," he explained, and to be sure I understood, he pointed to the policeman who had fired it who was also grinning broadly. "To alert Marines that we are approaching their perimeter. Not like last night!"

Sheepishly, I resumed my place in the column while the men tried to hide their grins. A quarter mile on, we encountered the Marines, now deployed in a perimeter around the hamlet.

We filed into the hamlet past neat thatch houses, and the policemen fanned out along the narrow lanes. The community was coming to life. Cooking fires were started. People moved about on early-morning tasks, drawing water from the well, or squatting and empting their bowels in an adjoining rice paddy.

Policemen went to each house. Householders presented their Family Census booklet and invited the policemen in to search and check identities of the occupants. The young Vietnamese policemen were polite, businesslike, but sensitive to the daybreak tasks of the villagers.

Using canes fashioned from steel reinforcing rods with a sharpened end, the police probed the roots of trees and piles of rubble, searching for spider holes that could conceal a Viet Cong soldier or a weapon.

It was not at all the scene press reports back home had conditioned me to expect of a police force isolated from the people, bullying and looting the population. Instead, I was impressed by their professionalism.

"Thiếu tá Anh," a housewife called to Major Anh and offered us each a bowl of noodles.

"Cảm ơn Bà," I managed. Standing in the lane, I ate the noodles with chopsticks and drank the broth from the bowl. Sometime during

the night, I had stopped thinking about the dog meat stuck in my gullet, and I was hungry. The soup was delicious, and I pledged to make *phò* my breakfast for at least the remainder of my time in Vietnam, if not forever.

Children appeared in the lanes. The boys dressed in blue shorts, white short-sleeved shirts, and white-plastic sun helmets. The girls wore white smocks and sunbonnets. The children carried plastic book bags that, given their diminutive stature, appeared to be the size of a suitcase.

Teenage girls wore white *ao dais* and conical straw hats. Their long, straight, black hair fell to their waist. Their backs to me as they walked down the footpath to school, they reminded me of penguins. The young policemen flirted with them, and the girls flirted back. It was such a stunningly normal scene that for a while I forgot the clamorous firefight in the dark that could have taken my life.

We did not find the machine gun that had fired at the jet aircraft during the night, nor did we find anyone the police could immediately identify as Viet Cong. The police did locate five young men, not listed in family census booklets, who claimed to be merely visiting friends or family in the village. Without resisting, they were handcuffed and taken into custody.

"We will take them back to police headquarters and interrogate them," Major Anh said. "Their stories will be checked with officials in the villages where thcy claimed residence."

An old man, wearing a sun helmet and dressed in a white ao dai, was also arrested but not handcuffed. Even he seemed to take it in stride. I asked Major Anh about him.

"Economic crimes," he replied cryptically.

The police were finished by noon, and in the warm, midday sun, we filed back to the bridge. It seemed much smaller than it had in the dark, when muzzle flashes and ricocheting tracers had lit up its iron girders.

Underneath the bridge at the edge of the stream, women in conical hats, their black pajamas rolled up above their knees, harvested watercress. The wet cress was a brilliant Kelly green. The men bantered with them as we passed, and the women grinned and offered up handfuls of the green, leafy plant.

I thought of summer evenings in Wisconsin, of loading into our family car and driving out to Pier Springs to picnic and harvest water-cress in the clear, spring-fed pond, and felt a twinge of homesickness. The melancholia lasted until I drifted off to sleep late in the afternoon.

Major Anh, his deputy, and the author at the Cam Le bridge the morning after they survived a friendly fire incident involving US Marines.

5

"See the river down there?" The pilot of the Swiss-made, silver-and-blue Air America Porter pointed at the snake-like, brown channel just south of the airstrip at Tam Ky. "Watch out the window to your right." He banked the high-performance wing monoplane far over to the left, executing a sharp 180-degree turn, and dove to the runway. Bright pinpoints of light, tracer bullets, floated up towards us from the far side of the river.

"Happens every day," the pilot shouted into my popping ears. "We don't own the real estate on the other side of that river." It appeared that, other than the town itself, we owned little in the neighborhood at all, day or night. On the way down from Danang, we flew off the coastline, cutting inland across the coastal plain, and approaching Tam Ky at three thousand feet, higher than the maximum effective range of small arms fire.

Taxiing along the runway towards the open shelter that served as a terminal, I noted the destroyed carcass of a civilian, two-engine, prop-driven aircraft, a C-47, reposing on its belly on the far side of the paved airstrip. It had been pulled off the runway to make way for other aircraft, I supposed, and become a permanent display.

Earl Harris, the departing USAID Office of Public Safety advisor, met me on the tarmac, and we made our way into town on a road clogged with trishaws, cyclos (motorized trishaws), motorbikes, and pedestrians. Oblivious to our approaching Jeep, peasants dressed in black pajamas and conical straw hats shuffled along the asphalt roadway balancing tote poles on their shoulders. Wicker baskets suspended from the ends of the poles were loaded with green produce, bags of rice, live chickens and pigs in bamboo cages, building materials, even small children. Occasionally, a dog lounging on the warm pavement in our path reluctantly rose to his feet and moved aside, but only when Earl revved the engine.

"Does no good to honk," Earl remarked. "These people are used to oxcarts, not cars."

"What'd they tell you in Danang?" Earl asked after a pause.

"That you're going home, and I'll be your replacement," I replied cautiously, sensing that the subject might be a little testy. At a too brief meeting in Danang that morning, I learned that I would be responsible not just for the National Police Field Force, as I had expected, but also the entire USAID Public Safety program in Quang Tin Province.

"Yeah, I'm ready to go," Earl replied. "I'll show you what I can, but I'm out of here day after tomorrow."

Confucian temple in Tam Ky.

I'd have a scant two days to pick up the reins in the broader National Police program, as well as the province prison and police telecommunications, activities for which I had little preparation. For the latter, Earl told me, I was inheriting a team of Filipino and Korean third country nationals, TCNs, hired by USAID to install and maintain the system.

We approached an intersection with what appeared to be the main street of Tam Ky. Earl said it was Route 1, the main north-south artery of South Vietnam. A policeman in a white shirt and grey trousers and cap, standing on a pedestal fashioned from a steel drum, swiveled one way and then another, futilely waving his arms and blowing his whistle as indifferent pedestrians and motorcyclists pushed past him from all directions at once.

Clear of the main business district of one- and two-story stucco buildings and open-air markets, we turned off Route 1 toward the province headquarters. Moving slowly in front of us, a large military dump truck with tandem, dual wheels competed for space on the pavement amidst the throng of pedestrians that now included children on their way home from school.

I casually watched a large, twin-rotor helicopter setting down in an open field next to the road that appeared to serve as both a parade ground and a heli-pad. Without warning, we were engulfed in a cloud of dirt and debris thrown up by the chopper's rotor wash.

In front of us, red taillights flashed. The dump truck jerked to an abrupt halt. Shouting excitedly, peasants dropped their totes and flocked to the rear of the truck. On the asphalt pavement just behind the truck's huge dual wheels lay the crushed body of a schoolboy, his plastic sun helmet and books strewn along the shoulder of the road.

Earl and I got out of our Jeep and rushed to the boy. Two stunned American Seabees climbed down from the cab of their truck. But there was nothing any of us could do.

The boy looked to be about ten or eleven, his mouth open wide as if he died in the middle of a scream, surprise, and terror frozen on his face for eternity. The villagers who had flocked to his aid pulled his white shirt up to his armpits, baring his belly, which was split open in a gash straight enough to be the work of a surgeon's scalpel. Feces squeezed from his bowels by the huge wheels strung along the back of his bare leg below his blue shorts. The boy had been running across the road to get a piece of candy from the chopper crew, but blinded by the stinging prop wash, he had not seen the truck.

Any notion I harbored of romantic death in a country at war was dashed forever. The boy's demise was random, ugly, and the waste of the youth's life.

From left to right: Bà Mui, the author's secretary; Cô Hai, Hoang's fiancée; Hoang, the author's interpreter; and Hoang's father.

Impatient, Earl insisted we move on. Pushing past the accident scene, we pulled up at the National Police headquarters a short distance away, a tropical-style, single-story, tan-stucco building. Louvered green shutters framed the unglazed windows. The Public Safety office occupied a single room in a front corner of the building.

At the office door, Earl introduced me to Hua Thi Mui, a slender woman about thirty who wore a bright, flower-print ao dai and matching hairband. Married, she nevertheless wore her kinky, black hair down over her shoulders. She had a wide mouth, and her eyes twinkled mischievously.

"Welcome, Mr. Harpold," she said in a coarse, almost masculine voice. "Hoang and I are happy you are here. You call me Bà Mui. I learn English from US Navy in Danang," she added proudly.

Next, Earl introduced me to Nguyen Huu Hoang, a slender youth in his twenties who wore a white, silky shirt, tight-fitting pants, and pointed shoes. His shiny, black hair was combed in an Elvis Presley pompadour. I extended my hand, which he clasped in both of his. He spoke very good English.

We had barely finished introductions when a stocky Vietnamese Army officer brusquely entered the room. Earl introduced him as

Captain Ha, the chief of the National Police in Quang Tin Province, and my new counterpart.

"Chào, Đại úy *Ha,"* I said, *"mạnh giỏi không?"*

Captain Ha spoke little more English than I did Vietnamese, and once past the pleasantries, Hoang interpreted. But it was soon clear that Earl and Captain Ha disliked each other, and the meeting was brief.

"C'mon, I need to introduce you to the province senior advisor, Lieutenant Colonel Bolté," Earl said. We picked our way through a barbed-wire barricade that protected the grounds surrounding province headquarters and crossed in front of the modestly grandeur stucco building to the single-story, wood-frame headquarters of MACV/CORDS Advisory Team #16.[1] Earl ushered me into the office of the Deputy PSA, Jerry Dobbs. Dobbs was a stout, florid-faced, retired army colonel, who now worked for USAID.

"I see that you're taking over from Earl," Dobbs said after we shook hands. "Have you had any military training?"

"Five years in the army," I said, "including a year and a half at West Point."

Dobbs grunted. "Has he been to the USAID compound yet?" he asked Earl.

"Not yet," Earl said.

"The Public Safety advisor is in charge at the USAID compound," Dobbs explained. "That was Earl's job, and now it's yours. That's because they're generally the only ones who have ever fired a gun before they got here. The other advisors are professors, ministers, a public health guy, and such. You've got an indigenous guard force, Nung, but I've never trusted men who fight for money. That's part of the reason the Americans have to be prepared to fight, too."

We went next to Colonel Bolté's office. "What do you know about Quang Tin Province?" he asked after Earl introduced me.

"Very little," I admitted.

Colonel Bolté escorted us next door to the province Tactical Operations Center, the TOC. The small, windowless, heavily sandbagged building was outfitted with an array of radio and communication

1. Military Assistance Command Vietnam/Civil Operations and Revolutionary Development Support, (MACV/CORDS) was the amalgam of military and civil assistance to the Government of Vietnam (GVN). At each level of government—regional, provincial, and district—US military and civilian advisors were embedded as counterparts to Vietnamese officials.

systems. A half-dozen Vietnamese and US Army officers manned lit-up panels and consoles in the dark interior.

"This is the province nerve center," Colonel Bolté explained. "We have commo with all the Regional Forces and Popular Forces in the province, as well as the Army of Vietnam, ARVN, and US military units. We can even call in fire support from US Navy ships off shore."

"How about the police?" I asked. Colonel Bolté looked at me quizzically. I took it there was none and made a mental note to look into why.

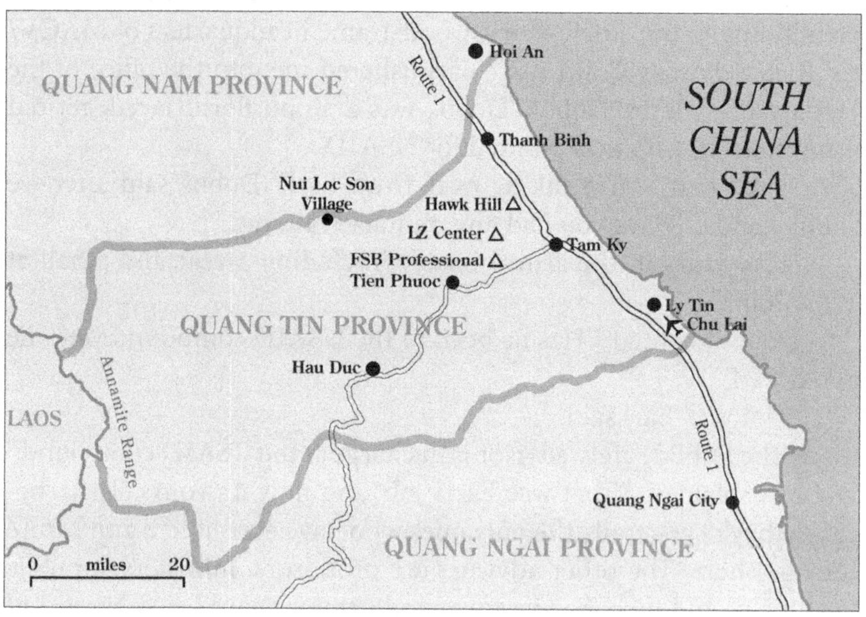

Quang Tin Province

Colonel Bolté pulled aside a curtain revealing a large-scale wall map of Quang Tin Province. The province extended from the spine of the Annamite Range, the Laotian border, to the South China Sea, a distance of about seventy miles. The capital, Tam Ky, with a population of about forty thousand, was situated in the rice-producing coastal plain astride Route 1. Two district capitols, Ly Tin to the south and Thang Binh to the north, were linked to Tam Ky by the mostly paved, two-lane highway.

"Barbed-wire barricades close off the road each night at the city limits," the colonel explained. "At dawn, mine-clearing teams, working on foot, clear the roadway north and south from town, a task generally not complete until late in the morning."

"This is Tien Phuoc," Colonel Bolté said pointing to a town in the foothills of the Annamites about twenty air miles west of Tam Ky. "It's a district town, but it was cut off from Tam Ky by the North Vietnamese Army—the NVA—four years ago. There's a Civilian Irregular Defense Group[2] unit there and a US Special Forces advisor. We've only recently been able to run biweekly armored supply convoys to it, but the security threat has been too great to do so this month."

Further west, Colonel Bolté pointed out the mountaintop town of Hau Duc. "It's cut off, too," he said. "You've got a police detachment out there, but you'll only be able to reach it by helicopter."

"This is Hiep Duc district," the colonel continued, pointing to an empty, dark-green area in the far west of the province bordering Laos. "It's all mountains and triple-canopy jungle and a sanctuary of the NVA. There has been no Government of Vietnam—GVN—presence there since the partition in 1954."

I noted numerous winding, dashed lines on the map, representing foot trails. Colonel Bolté pointed to the single set of double-dashed lines marking an unimproved road. It originated across the border in Laos but seemed to dead end in the jungle a few miles into Hiep Duc.

"This is Route 16, an abandoned French road that the NVA uses to connect to the Ho Chi Minh Trail," Colonel Bolté said. "They're trying to improve it. Photo recon shows the road now progresses nineteen miles into the province, one-quarter of the distance to Tam Ky. They're protecting it with anti-aircraft artillery, so it's important. Their plan is to take Tam Ky and push through to the coast, cutting the country in two.

"This is the area we're most concerned about at the moment," Colonel Bolté said, pointing to a cluster of low hills just west of the Tam Ky airstrip. I sensed we had come to the point of the briefing. "This used to be a tea plantation, and we know that a large NVA force, possibly three regiments, as many as ten thousand men, is building

2. Civilian Irregular Defense Group. The units, mostly Montagnards, were recruited and trained by the US Special Forces for guerilla warfare in the mountainous and border regions of South Vietnam.

up there." Colonel Bolté let the information sink in. The area was no more than two or three miles southwest of town.

"The USAID compound is pretty exposed out there on the edge of town," Colonel Bolté explained, turning to me. "There's an ARVN armored cavalry unit, the White Horse Squadron, not far from you, but Colonel Tho, the province chief, has got to be able to use them as a reaction force if the town is attacked. If we get in trouble, you'll be on your own.

"The closest US unit, the First Squadron of the First Cavalry Regiment, is based on Hawk Hill about thirty kilometers north of us. If road mines don't hold them up, they can get down here in about two hours. You'll have to hold out until then."

6

THE LATE AFTERNOON SUN DESCENDED towards the western horizon, highlighting the ridges of the Annamites against the ominous dark shadows that cloaked the slopes and valleys between them. Earl stopped for a moment at the intersection of a dirt road paralleling an abandoned railroad track. The air was still, foreboding; even the birds roosting in the scrub trees seemed to have stopped singing. Across the tracks, sparse savannah, a no-man's land, stretched towards the low hills of the abandoned tea plantation where Colonel Bolté said the North Vietnamese Army was preparing to attack the town of Tam Ky.

"The rail line used to run from Saigon to Hanoi," Earl explained. "It had to be abandoned because the Viet Cong kept blowing up the bridges."

We turned right, past a thatch house on the corner that Earl identified as a brothel run by the South Vietnamese Army, and immediately turned right again into a dirt driveway. About fifty yards in, a black, iron gate barred our way; on either side stood a ten-foot-high, concrete wall topped with concertina wire and security lights. A broad apron of barbwire extended out from the wall. Pegged into the ground beneath the wire, olive-green, curved-face bricks, deadly claymore mines, lay poised to cut swaths in the ranks of an attacker. Above the corners of the whitewashed wall and at the middle, perforated-metal sleeves of WWII era .30-caliber machine guns poked from sandbag emplacements.

"Welcome to your sweet home away from home," Earl quipped.

Grinning and saluting, a stocky, round-faced Asian wearing green fatigues swung open the gate.

"Is he Nung?" I asked.

"Yeah, we have about fifteen of them," Earl said. "They're good, and despite what Dobbs says, they are loyal. One of them was killed a week ago. That's Hau, their captain, and right away he's gonna want to talk to you about compensation, but he wants too much. If you give in to them, they're just gonna want more."

Earl parked against a large bunker partially dug into the ground and covered in even rows of dark-green sandbags. The snout of a 60 mm mortar protruded above the walls of a sandbag emplacement on the top.

The compound was about two hundred feet on a side. A cluster of four prefab duplexes housed eight of the American advisors, Earl said. He ushered me past the bunker and a water well to a white-washed masonry house with a pitched, red-tile roof. It appeared to have existed prior to USAID having built a compound around it. A small pagoda on a pedestal stood in front of the house, sheltering a small statue of Buddha. Burning joss gave off a wispy curl of smoke and an incense-like fragrance.

"The Nung use that," Earl said, and I picked up a note of disdain. "You'll have to share the back bedroom at least until I leave."

I threw my gear on the empty bed. The room had a window air-conditioning unit and a bath with a flush toilet and shower. *Good enough*, I thought. It was considerably more than I had expected.

Back outside, Earl led me across the compound to a warehouse inside the front gate and introduced me to Mr. Leung, a middle-aged Vietnamese man with slicked-back hair, wearing a white dress shirt and brown pants. He spoke good English.

"Mr. Leung takes care of the upkeep around here and the house-keeping stuff," Earl said. "He hires all the maids and workers, including the guards."

Two Nung approached us through the open warehouse door. Mr. Leung introduced Captain Hau, who he said was the chief of the Nung.

"Chào dai uy Hau," I said formally. Grinning broadly, he took my outstretched hand and shook it vigorously.

"He doesn't speak Vietnamese, only Chinese," Mr. Leung explained. "His companion, Moui, translates for him, but Moui doesn't speak English, only Vietnamese and Chinese."

Wow! I thought. *How's this going to work when we get in a pinch?*

Captain Hau immediately engaged Mr. Leung in an earnest conversation through Moui that I could not follow. Mr. Leung turned to me.

"He wants compensation for the guard that was killed at the airport," Mr. Leung said. "He knows Mr. Harris is leaving, and you're the new man in charge. He wants to know what you're going to do about it."

I looked at Earl.

"Last Sunday afternoon, we were at the firing range at the far end of the airport runway," Earl explained. "It's just an earthen berm, but we use it to teach the new guys to shoot and to fire our automatic weapons every couple months. A group of Vietnamese Popular Forces soldiers came down the runway behind us and started firing at us. We thought at first they were Viet Cong. The Nung charged them. One of the Nung was killed.

"Turned out the shooters were from the Popular Forces training camp on the far side of the runaway. They even had an American sergeant, their advisor, with them. They say they thought we were VC."

"So how's this supposed to work?" I asked Mr. Leung.

"USAID will give the man's wife three thousand dong," he replied.

I did some mental calculation and sucked in my breath. It was less than thirty dollars. Earl shrugged his shoulders.

"Tell Captain Hau that I am very sorry for the loss of his man, and I will look into it right away," I said to Mr. Leung. Apparently satisfied that their message had been received, after another round of handshakes and grins, the two Nung left.

"Seems pretty skimpy," I said to Mr. Leung. "What more can we do here?"

"We give the widow her husband's pay for a full month. I told Mr. Byrd, the administrative officer, and he agreed. More than that, I don't know."

"Can we employ the widow?" I asked. "I see several women working around here."

"Well, I don't know," Mr. Leong temporized. "The Vietnamese women might object. That is their work."

I vowed not to be deterred by Mr. Leong's objection. I recalled Colonel Dobb's comment earlier that afternoon that he didn't trust men who fought only for money. I thought about the incident at the NPFF training center in Dalat and the hair-trigger sensitivities of the Nung. They had fired on the Vietnamese trainees they were hired to protect. With an attack on the town imminent, I thought, *This is a helluva time to have a money dispute with men we need to defend us.*

Back outside, Earl introduced me to Bill Allen, a retired Marine and the province logistics advisor. A key man in the little American community, he was responsible for maintaining the two generators that provided electricity for the housing units and the perimeter lights. Bill led us to the back of the masonry house where two well-maintained generators stood on a concrete pad under a tin roof. Neatly lettered signs in Vietnamese and English laid out in numbered steps the daily, weekly, and monthly maintenance the machines required.

"These generators are critical because they power the perimeter lights," Bill said. "But, the biggest problem I have is these guys who buy these Japanese reel-to-reel tape decks, those Akais and TEACs that they pick up in Japan or Hong Kong that run on Asian, 50 cycle electricity." Bill looked me square in the eye, accusingly. "The generators are set to produce 60 cycle, but these guys get out here in the dark and tinker with them to get their music to sound right."

"I don't own a tape deck," I said defensively. "About the perimeter lights," I asked. "Don't they make us an easy target for indirect fire at night?"

"Every new guy asks that, and we've talked about it a lot," Bill answered. "According to some USAID bureaucrat back in Washington, we're supposed to hide down in there when we're being attacked," Bill said, gesturing to the sandbag-covered, bunker in the center of the compound. "If the bad guys get over the wall and we're all down in that bunker, a satchel charge or just one grenade would take all of us out. That's happened to other advisory teams. None of us wants to die hunkered down in a hole. We get up on the wall bunkers and fight alongside the Nung."

Peering into the dark interior, I saw a chamber about ten feet on a side. It was protected by two-foot-thick concrete walls and ceiling. Boxes of ammunition and medical equipment were stacked along the walls.

"During the dark phase of the moon, the VC are able to creep in close enough to hit us with mortars and rockets, sometimes even machine gunfire," Bill continued. "Last month, a Soviet 122 mm rocket hit right here in the center of the compound and dug a crater six foot deep. No one was hurt, but the concussion flattened every single tire on our vehicles."

I took the time to climb to the tops of the wall bunkers, each manned by a grinning Nung. The men lived with their families in the cramped, bottom story of the structures. Distributed between the five positions, I counted seven Browning automatic rifles and four .30-caliber machine guns, all WWII vintage weapons that according to Earl had been scrounged from the South Vietnamese Army.

That evening, Earl took me to the MACV compound to eat. It was on a nearby street but closer to the center of town. The compound housed the forty or so military advisors of MACV/CORDS Advisory Team 16, but the mess hall served both military and civilians.

At the table, Earl introduced me to Jim Daw, a stocky, young civilian with short blond hair, and explained that he was the advisor to the Chieu Hoi program.

"We convince captured Viet Cong to convert to the government side," Jim said.

He spoke more Vietnamese than I could thus far manage and volunteered to help me communicate with Captain Hau.

David Miller, who shared the masonry house with me, advised the province Revolutionary Development office, a joint US/Government of Vietnam program. The effort was heralded in the American press, but any sort of development was hard to achieve given the province's precarious security. Nevertheless, David worked at it with determination.

Gary Beyer, Gene Schiaparelli, and Carl Harris worked in refugee resettlement. Gary and Gene were Foreign Service officers, and Carl was a Unitarian minister from Philadelphia.

Dave Glennon, a heavyset man with great bushy eyebrows whose jowly face seemed permanently split by a grin, introduced himself as a de-frocked doctor from New York.

"Bác sĩ Dave," Carl Harris quipped. "He holds office hours every morning for the neighbors."

His work for pay as a USAID public health educator, Dave explained, was to persuade village councils to clean up their domestic water by building latrines.

"The people are immaculately clean about their bodies," he said, "but they have no conception of germs and disease being spread through their ground water."

Leroy Anderson, a tall, sandy-haired Scandinavian, a professor of agriculture at the University of Wisconsin, was the province agriculture and fisheries advisor. He had had a sheet of quarter-inch steel welded to the under frame of his International Scout as protection from land mines as he made his way among the paddy fields.

After dinner, we adjourned to a couple of tables in the small club next to the mess hall.

I ordered a Scotch and water but was told the only hard liquor the club sold was crème de menthe.

"The club gets supplied one pallet at a time of just one type of liquor," Gary explained. "We have to drink up the crème de menthe before we can get something else."

"All right," I said, understanding I needed to do my bit but wondering how many months it would take fifty men to drink one hundred cases of the syrupy, green liqueur. "Crème de menthe on the rocks."

I brought up the subject of the dead Nung, repeating what Mr. Leung had said about compensation for the widow. "Thirty dollars doesn't sound like much to me," I said.

"The problem is that he's on the payroll as a gardener," Ralph Byrd said. A small, wiry man, he was an accountant and kept track of USAID program funds allocated to the province and the local employee payroll. "USAID authorizes us only eight guards. We have fifteen, and so we pay the others as maids and laborers. Three thousand dong is what a gardener's family would get if he had a heart attack raking up leaves."

"That's not right," Dave Glennon said, "particularly when he died defending us." Retrieving his wallet, he threw a wad of piasters on the table. One by one, the others followed suit until at the end of the evening we had collected over thirty thousand dong and pledges for ten thousand more, about four hundred dollars.

"What about hiring the widow, putting her on our payroll?" I asked. The amount of cash still seemed a little short, and the proposal provoked some thought.

"She can be my maid," Dave Miller spoke up.

"We can share her," Jim Daw added. "I don't mind."

Ralph Byrd agreed with the arrangement, and with that, I was confident Mr. Leung would go along, too. I would turn over the money we had collected to Captain Hau first thing in the morning. But on the way back to the USAID compound, Earl disagreed one more time.

"Mike, everything you try to do for these people over here has a consequence," he pointed out. "You're replacing a Vietnamese maid with a Nung, and that will have repercussions, too."

I sensed Earl was right, but he was leaving. I was responsible now, and I had to be clear-eyed about the situation. I had no intention of opening a grievance with men who we might soon depend upon for our lives, even if they were mercenaries.

That night, I was jolted upright in bed by a series of close-by explosions. I grabbed my flak jacket, rifle, and helmet, and in nothing but my trousers rushed barefoot out into the rain. None of the other Americans had stirred. I stood in the middle of the compound alone, perplexed. The Nung on watch in the wall bunkers discretely looked away. Jim Daw, the duty officer that night, had been sleeping on the screen porch of his prefab and came to my aid.

"That's outgoing," he explained. "There's a battery of South Vietnamese eight-inch guns behind us, and apparently they've received a fire mission. Most nights, they just randomly lob shells out in the jungle for harassment and interdiction. You'll learn to sleep through it."

The following night, I was awakened by shots fired by one of the Nung. Rushing outside, I found the compound in total darkness. A steady rain was falling. This time, I was not alone; I saw the shapes of

Americans wearing flak vests and steel helmets over their underwear or pajamas clambering to positions in the wall bunkers.

"We've got a power outage," Jim Daw explained. "We have to stay on alert until we get the lights back on again."

I found Bill Allen at the top of a ladder cursing drunkenly. A flashlight in hand, he examined the wire that ran along the top of the wall to the perimeter lights, soon locating a household electric cord spliced into the line. Climbing another step or two, he braced his knees against the ladder and yanked. There was a terrific clatter as a lamp, toaster, and a radio were pulled through the thatch wall of the house a Vietnamese family had built against the outside of the wall. I climbed up behind Bill and held the light while he patched the bared wires. Shortly, our perimeter lights came on again.

We started back to our rooms but not before I got a glimpse at the arms the advisors were equipped with: military 12-gauge shotguns, WWII M-1 rifles, pre-war Thompson submachine guns.

"Scrounged from the ARVN," Jim Daw explained, noticing my interest.

I heaved a sigh, Colonel Bolté's warning ringing through my head: *If we get in trouble, you'll have to hold out on your own.*

7

THE NEXT AFTERNOON, THREE DAYS AFTER I ARRIVED in Tam Ky, a squadron of M-48 tanks and M-114 armored personnel carriers of the South Vietnamese White Horse Squadron, probing the ruined tea plantation for the North Vietnamese unit suspected to have infiltrated into the area, came under intense fire. Colonel Bolté was with the unit and immediately called for backup from the US First Squadron of the First Cavalry Regiment. A troop returning from a battle near Quang Ngai, one hundred kilometers south through Tam Ky to its base on Hawk Hill, diverted to join the developing fray. Such intense rocket-propelled grenade fire met the armored vehicles that they could not proceed, and by nightfall, a stalemate ensued.

Flushed out before they could begin their attack, the North Vietnamese were deprived of the element of surprise. Nonetheless, that night they pressed their attack on Tam Ky, overrunning the airport and fighting their way into a neighborhood south of the USAID compound, destroying five hundred houses. As we watched from our positions on our front wall, fiery, orange mushrooms rose from the hilltops to the southwest. Fighter-bombers and Spooky gunships rained napalm and bullets down on the main body of enemy troops.[1] The eight-inch guns behind us fired furiously. Rolling down Route 1 from their base on Hawk Hill, thirty kilometers to the north, additional units of the First of the First clanked into town.

---

1. Spooky gunships were WWII era two-engine transport airplanes, later C-123s or C-130s, with one or two Gatling guns mounted in side windows capable of putting a bullet into every square foot of ground in a fifty-yard swath beneath their flight path.

Shoulder to shoulder with the Nung, we manned our fighting positions on the walls of the USAID compound, watching anxiously. Sporadically, a mortar shell exploded in the soft soil in or near the compound, sending a geyser of dirt into the air, but causing little damage.

Tank of the US First Battalion of the First Armored Cavalry Regiment on a Tam Ky street. They often rode to the town's rescue from their base on Hawk Hill twenty miles north.

A little after two in the morning, a platoon of tanks and armored fighting vehicles, ACAVs, crept along the dirt road in front of the USAID compound, turning and taking positions along the railroad tracks. The creak and clank of the tracks were as reassuring as the clarion call of a cavalryman's bugle of an earlier era. We cheered heartily.

Early in the assault, a North Vietnamese battalion commander was captured along with the enemy plan of attack. Knowing every Communist maneuver in advance, the South Vietnamese and US armored vehicles positioned themselves accordingly, mowing down ranks of the attackers. The battle became a turkey shoot.

After three days of heavy fighting, the North Vietnamese fell back, leaving behind 296 of their dead. The USAID compound had been spared a direct assault but had been hit by a half-dozen, seemingly random, mortar shells. The shells exploded in the soft soil, both inside and outside the walls, throwing up geysers that showered us with shrapnel and dirt. Crouching in our sandbagged fighting positions, protected by flak vests and steel helmets, no American or Nung had been hurt.

Despite the pitched battle raging on the outskirts of the town, I was astonished to see Vietnamese children lining the streets each morning and afternoon on their way to and from school. Seated in rows at long wooden desks in open-windowed schoolhouses, they recited their lessons in unison, seemingly oblivious to the explosions, the crack of rifle fire, and the staccato pop of machine guns emanating on the western outskirts of the town and clearly audible in the background. Hoang and Mui were at my office in police headquarters each morning despite the fighting close to their homes. War aside, life in Tam Ky simply went on.

Despite Tam Ky being under siege, children still went to school.

During the day, we went about our jobs, too. The refugee program advisors—Gene, Gary, and Carl—had their hands full helping their Vietnamese counterparts house and feed hundreds of refugees displaced by the fighting or who had sought safety in the town.

Dave Glennon worked tirelessly at the province hospital, assisting the US Navy surgeon and the Vietnamese doctor, treating wounded survivors from the neighborhood overrun by the North Vietnamese on the first night of the battle. No one asked to see his medical license. When he got a break and returned to his quarters, wounded and sick Vietnamese came to the compound asking to see Bác sĩ Dave and lined up outside his door, waiting for wounds to be dressed, bandages to be changed, anti-biotics to be administered.

I went with Captain Ha to check strong points and barricades the police manned in the city to interdict infiltrators. The NPFF was deployed in positions surrounding province and police headquarters but had not seen action.

I checked in often with the prison chief, Mr. Dang. In an assault on the town in May, the North Vietnamese and VC attackers managed to free over three hundred prisoners. This time, Colonel Tho augmented the defense of the fortress-like building with a Regional Forces company.

Each night, we returned to our bunkers and our weapons, dozing at our posts, glimpsing at the light show to the southwest of us as Vietnamese and US armored vehicles and aircraft pummeled the North Vietnamese troops.

The North Vietnamese battalion commander, Colonel Nguyen Nguyen, who had been captured in possession of the Communist battle plan, told his captors that he wanted to renounce North Vietnam and become a returnee, a *hoi chanh*. He proved to be an amiable fellow and quickly became a local hero, although it would be four more months of re-education in the Chieu Hoi center before he could be freed into the local population. Colonel Tho showed him around town. Jim Daw had participated in the interrogation and was feted along with the former Communist commander at a dinner at the province chief's residence.

On the first day after Route #1 was reopened, a tank truck arrived from Danang with a load of smolt imported by USAID. Before the attack, agriculture advisor Leroy Anderson had persuaded Colonel Tho to build a dike in a bend of the river to create a pond for a fish hatchery. After watching the small fish being pumped into the pond, we retired to the MACV club and toasted Leroy's success with a round of crème de menthe.

In the meantime, Captain Ha had been anxious about his men in Tien Phuoc, the district town in the foothills about twenty miles west of Tam Ky in the direct path of the North Vietnamese assault against Tam Ky. After the Communists retreated and the airfield was again secure, Captain Ha and I flew to Tien Phuoc in a four-seat Helio Courier I chartered from Air America. I brought Hoang also.

The district chief and the chief of the National Police met us at the Tien Phuoc airstrip, but Hoang immediately went to a clutch of people who were attending a middle-aged woman heavily bandaged on her face and neck.

"Mr. Harpold, this is the mother of my fiancé, Hai," Hoang said returning to the aircraft, holding the woman by the arm. "She was hurt by a mortar explosion. She needs to go to the hospital in Tam Ky." I had met Cô Hai in Tam Ky, a pretty teenager with perfect features, who like Hoang, wore western clothes typical of young Americans.

"Do you have others who need medical attention?" I asked the police chief. In areas protected by US forces, the army provided medical care, often evacuating injured civilians to US field hospitals. But in Tien Phuoc, there was only a Regional Forces company and a force of Montagnards with a Green Beret advisor to protect the town and no US medical facility, only a small government dispensary. Cut off by road, my small aircraft was the only way for injured civilians to get to a hospital.

"Many," the chief explained. "The NVA are retreating, but they are still all around us, and they raid us for food and medicine."

I had planned that the Helio would return to Tam Ky and shuttle rice and men to Tien Phuoc while Captain Ha and I did our business, but it was now apparent that the Helio pilot was going to have a full day.

We walked to a local café for lunch, a thatch building with a hard-packed dirt floor. A water glass filled with wooden chopsticks and a spindle of small, square paper napkins stood at the center of each of the three or four small tables. I followed the lead of Captain

Ha, Hoang, and the local police chief, selecting a pair of wooden chopsticks, ensuring they were straight and of equal length by tapping them on the bare, wooden tabletop and vigorously wiping them with a paper napkin. I was glad I had had hepatitis shots.

The proprietor's wife set rice bowls, teacups, and a steaming pot of tea before us. Again following the lead of my companions, I swirled hot tea in my teacup, dumped it into my rice bowl, swirled again, and then emptied it onto the dirt floor.

The woman brought sauce dishes containing sliced, red-hulled peppers immersed in an amber, foul-smelling sauce. My companions picked up a slice with their chopsticks and popped it into their mouths.

"*Nước mắm*," Captain Ha, said. "Fish sauce. Try it."

I had been warned about *nước mắm*; the sauce, a delicacy in the Vietnamese diet, was collected from rotting fish. Steeling myself against the appalling stench, I popped a pepper into my mouth. My lips burned, and a sip of tea did not quench the fire.

The food came: a heaping bowl of steaming rice, a platter of chopped-up chicken, and a platter of greens. I had been warned in advance by Dave Glennon to avoid green, leafy vegetables, and I did. They were grown in fields where the ground water was heavily polluted by human waste, virtually every field in Vietnam.

I filled my bowl with the sticky rice, and with my chopsticks picked up a piece of chicken, draining the juices on my rice, and popped it into my mouth. I was able to separate the meat from the gristle and bone with my tongue and teeth easily enough. With my chopsticks, I returned the scraps neatly to my rice bowl. I looked sideways at Hoang and Captain Ha but was startled to see that they spit the bones on the dirt floor. A dog policed them up.

I took another piece of chicken, but I was unable to bring myself to spit the remains on the floor. Again, the remnants went into my rice bowl. Soon, a collection of bones, fat, and gristle covered my rice. As discretely as I could manage, I removed the detritus from the bowl and placed it on the table, covering the pile with one of the tiny napkins. Conversation quieted while my companions studiously attended to their rice bowls.

Able to access my rice once again, I seasoned it with soy sauce and continued eating. I decided to try a piece of chicken again, popping one of the few remaining morsels, more gristle and bone than meat, into my mouth. When I finished, I turned my head and spit, *patooie!* The remnants shot to the floor. My companions grinned broadly. Conversation resumed.

"Did you not like the food?" Captain Ha asked when we had finished. He was staring into my rice bowl at the half dozen grains of rice I had been unable to capture with the blunt ends of my chopsticks.

"Yes, yes," I protested. "*Nó là rất tốt.* It was very delicious."

I heard my mother's voice from afar: *Clean your plate, Michael! What will people think of you when you grow up?* Twenty-five years later and half a world away, Captain Ha had just said as much.

8

I GLANCED AROUND THE TABLE, TALLYING each man who had yet to rise and sing a song, recite a poem, or perform a magic trick, realizing with increasing panic that soon it would be my turn. I couldn't even sing "Happy Birthday," such was my lack of talent.

Not realizing that participatory entertainment was customary after such an event, or that I would be expected to be a part of it, I was surprised when at the end of the meal Captain Ha, my counterpart and the host for the evening, rose and sang a Vietnamese folk song. As I struggled to come up with something, old Mr. Thieu, the deputy police chief, unwittingly gave me a few extra minutes of cover as he recited long verses of Vietnam's epic poem. I thought of telling a story, but few of the dozen police and province officials at the table spoke or understood English.

I kicked myself for not asking to bring Hoang, my interpreter. Coming just a week after US and South Vietnamese armored cavalry forces had saved Tam Ky, the dinner was a delayed welcome to Tam Ky.

The affair had started with "33" Export and platters of hors d'oeuvres, small birds, their feathers charred away, their tiny head and toothpick like legs protruding from the toasted carcass.

"Cái nây là gì?" I asked Captain Ha.

"Chim," he replied. "Little bird boiled live in *mia,* sugarcane. Very good. You try."

After fortifying myself with another swallow of beer, I picked up one of the bite-sized morsels by the leg and boldly popped it in my mouth. The bones had been softened in the boiling cane sugar, but

I experienced an unnerving moment when the tiny skull crunched between my molars.

When we were seated, steaming dishes were brought from the kitchen and arrayed on large lazy Susans. Captain Ha ceremoniously presented me the delicacy, the head of something resting on a bed of crispy noodles. An eye stared up at me. The tiny sugarcane swallows were one thing, but I was not about to bite into the head of a pigeon. My face frozen into a grin of appreciation, I intuitively passed the plate to Mr. Thieu, whom I perceived to be the oldest man at the table. My fellow diners gasped in admiration and then applauded. Mr. Thieu smiled and bowed while silently I sighed in relief.

Another song and another poem, and it was my turn. I struggled to my feet, suffering a moment of agoraphobia as suddenly I towered above the men at the table. They applauded me enthusiastically, expectantly.

"*Ngày xửa ngày xưa ở Việt Nam có một người thợ săn tên Trương sống ở trong rừng*" (a long time ago in ancient Vietnam, a hunter named Trương lived in the forest), I managed in Vietnamese, my knees shaking. I had learned the folk tale from the cultural secretary at the Vietnamese embassy in Washington, DC, who regularly visited our language class at the Foreign Service Institute on Friday afternoons. With only the back-of-the-mind thought that I would ever recite it in front of an audience, I had obtained a copy in Vietnamese more as a study aid and had begun to memorize it. But the story was lengthy and complex, and I knew I could not yet recite more than a few lines of it in Vietnamese. I prayed for a miracle.

"Trương was having very bad luck, and his family was hungry," I continued, striving to get the right words and speak the tones correctly. The men listened attentively but looked puzzled. I could sense that few, if any, understood.

"One day, Trương came upon a brown snake who was being attacked by a black snake. Trương slew the black snake with an arrow." I wove my hands to imitate the battle between the snakes and then pantomimed the hunter shooting the fatal arrow. "That night, the brown snake came to Trương's cabin and offered him a magic black pearl that gave him the power to talk to the animals."

"He puts the pearl under his tongue!" Captain Ha interrupted, gesturing to his mouth.

My miracle had arrived. Relieved, I turned and applauded Captain Ha who rose and repeated the story to that point in Vietnamese.

"You say," he said, urging me to continue. "I help."

Between us, with a great deal more of pantomime on my part, we finished the tale. The diners leapt to their feet, applauding wildly. Captain Ha ordered another bottle of Martel for the table.

Coming only nights after the rout of the North Vietnamese force that had attacked Tam Ky, the dinner was a manifestation of relief as much as it was my welcoming. As it had in two other assaults earlier in the year, the Tet offensive in January and Mini-Tet in May, the town bent but had not broken.

9

THROUGH BINOCULARS, I EXAMINED THE CLUSTER of thatch houses the province chief said was the source of Viet Cong sniper fire on travelers on Route 1. The hamlet sat on a small knoll isolated by floodwaters that covered even the tops of the banks surrounding the rice paddies. I could spot no activity. It could be abandoned because of the rising water, I thought, but that didn't mean there were no VC hiding there.

We needed to find out, but first we had to find a way for a National Police Field Force platoon to get across the three-hundred-yard wide expanse of water. I was already wet from the monsoon rain, but I stepped from the bank onto the top of a submerged dike anyway. The cold water gushed through the vents in the instep of my jungle boots and rose on my calves.

"It's not too deep for your men," I called to Lieutenant Tam, the NPFF commander. "You can see the top of the dike." But he didn't budge. I waded in knee-deep water to a point about a dozen yards from the shore, but Lieutenant Tam, as if posing for a photo of himself, remained implacable on the bank, his legs spread, jaw thrust forward, hands on his hips, in the vogue created by the flamboyant Vietnamese vice president and fighter pilot, Nguyen Cao Ky. He sported a revolver slung low off his right hip, cowboy style. Despite the rain, he wore dark, aviator glasses.

Hoang had told me that Lieutenant Tam was only nineteen years old, the son of a wealthy Saigon family who were connected enough to buy him a commission in the army and an assignment to the National

Police where they felt there would be less danger. In contrast to the brown camouflage uniforms worn by his men, he sported, expensive, green-and-black, tiger-stripe cammies. A black beret pulled down to his eyebrows was his sole concession to the NPFF uniform. Bà Mui said that while watching an American cowboy movie in the crowded local cinema, he drew his pistol and fired a bullet into the ceiling.

Earlier that morning, Lieutenant Tam had come to my office to tell me about the snipers. The province chief, Colonel Tho, had given him twenty-four hours to clean them out. I had been in Tam Ky just two weeks. Pressed with the business of the North Vietnamese attack—protecting the prison, which housed seven hundred VC and NVA prisoners had been a high priority—I had not had much time to acquaint myself with the NPFF company or Lieutenant Tam. I asked him to take me to reconnoiter the site, which was about two miles north of Tam Ky.

"Mr. Harpold," Lieutenant Tam said as I rejoined him on the sodden bank, "it will be safer if we go before dawn so the VC can't see us, but in the dark we won't be able to see the tops of the dikes. Besides, there's a river out there somewhere." A subordinate passed me a contour map, and hidden under the floodwaters but marked by a blue line was a river.

"Then we'll have to use boats," I replied patiently.

"We don't have any boats," Lieutenant Tam said. I didn't expect that the police did, but amid the myriad military units in Tam Ky, there was bound to be one or two we could borrow.

Rooting out the snipers in the water-bound hamlet was a classic paramilitary police function, but I was beginning to realize that I would have to take Lieutenant Tam by the hand to get the job done. I wondered if the real reason he sought my help was not to assist him and his men to plan and execute the mission but to enlist me to persuade Colonel Tho to cancel it.

The province chief was a blustery Vietnamese army officer who, at the farewell function he threw for Colonel Bolté, wasted little time in letting me know his low opinion of the National Police, particularly the NPFF. Before he left, my predecessor, Earl Harris, told me Colonel Tho had wanted to use the NPFF as his "palace guard." The province headquarters, including Colonel Tho's quarters, had been partially overrun by the NVA during the Tet offensive. Saigon authorities said that was not the role of the National Police and had rebuffed him. The Colonel blamed Lieutenant Tam's family connections.

The search for a boat led us to the Tam Ky district chief, a young, bookish-looking official dressed in black pajamas. He offered us a Boston Whaler, a flat-bottomed boat able to carry a dozen armed police at a time. It was the best we could muster on such short notice.

"We'll need a truck to carry the boat," Lieutenant Tam pointed out when we climbed back into his Jeep.

"That shouldn't be a problem," I said. The National Police had a five-ton GMC truck that to the best I could see sat mostly idle. "We can ask Captain Ha."

"But the highway won't be open until about 9 a.m., after daylight," Lieutenant Tam persisted. "We would have no chance for surprise."

My exasperation growing, I asked Lieutenant Tam to drive us to the Tactical Operations Center. In the small, darkened room, I explained the proposed operation to the US and Vietnamese officers responsible for coordinating military operations within the province.

"Yes, it would be hazardous to take a truck on the highway before it was cleared of mines, but personnel are not apt to trigger a pressure mine," an American captain said. "You could truck the Whaler to the edge of town and carry it the rest of the way. It's only a mile or two."

Lieutenant Tam was dismayed, but I reminded him that he himself had said crossing the flooded paddies before dawn would be less hazardous than if we waited for daylight. We returned to police headquarters, and Captain Ha readily gave us the use of the police five-ton truck.

Clearly, the operation would be complex and dangerous, but I was not ready to conclude that the province chief was being unreasonable. Suppressing VC snipers threatening military and civilian traffic on Route #1 was a sound reason for the operation, and it was clearly within the mission and the capabilities of the NPFF to carry out. I suspected also that Colonel Tho viewed it as a test for both Lieutenant Tam and me. I had no intention of leading the operation; that was Lieutenant Tam's job, but it was clear I would have to accompany him or it wouldn't happen at all.

We agreed on a jump-off time of five the following morning, but after Lieutenant Tam and I parted that afternoon, I began in earnest to struggle with my own fears. If things went wrong, we were certain to wind up in the water. I was not much of a swimmer, certainly not a strong enough one to keep my head above water weighted down by a heavy flak jacket and combat gear. A non-swimmer when I entered West Point, I had barely passed survival swimming and had swum few times since.

I didn't sleep that night; there were so many things that could go wrong in the morning. I didn't know if the fully loaded Boston Whaler would clear the submerged levies or if we would have to wade out on the narrow tops of the dikes in the dark and climb into the boat at the un-seeable edge of the flooded river. If we didn't achieve surprise, while attempting to cross the three hundred yards of open water, we'd be sitting ducks for sniper fire. Success or failure, possibly our lives, would rest on the resourcefulness of men who I had never been with in the field. Worse, I had no faith in Lieutenant Tam. I got out of bed and practiced unzipping and shrugging out of my flak vest in the event I wound up in the water.

Two hours before dawn, I was still awake. I got up, donned my field gear, and drove to the assembly point near the downtown market. The light-green police GMC five-ton truck was parked on the street, the Boston Whaler already loaded in the vehicle's canopied bed. Police wearing flak jackets and helmets and armed with carbines milled in the cold pre-dawn drizzle. Hoang joined me. Lieutenant Tam assured us that as soon as all his men arrived, we'd be ready to go.

It started to rain harder, and police not already in the truck pulled ponchos over their heads. Hoang and I waited in my Jeep. Fifteen, then thirty, minutes passed. I sent Hoang to find the reason for the delay.

"The driver is not here, and no one else has the keys to the truck," Hoang reported when he returned.

"What?" I said, dumbstruck.

"The driver parked it here last night and went home. Lieutenant Tam sent a man to his house to find him."

I was chagrined, but there was nothing to do but wait further. Another half-hour passed, and still the truck didn't move. Dawn approached, grey, and rainy; this time I went with Hoang to find out what was going on.

"Mr. Harpold, we can't find the keys to the truck," Lieutenant Tam pleaded. "The man who parked it here last night went home, and now no one can find him."

"Look," I yelled, out of patience. "I'm not the one who's going to have to explain to Colonel Tho that you couldn't get this done! That's going to be YOUR job!"

The sky was light when Lieutenant Tam sent a subordinate to tell me that Colonel Tho had called off the operation. I learned later that Lieutenant Tam went to Captain Ha, and the hapless police chief was the one who had to tell the storming province chief that the operation had to be cancelled because the NPFF couldn't find the keys to the truck.

I was exasperated, embarrassed; yet I had to admit to myself that I felt a great sense of relief. Going into an armed encounter at a tactical disadvantage, with the possibility of losing the cover of darkness and the element of surprise, led by an immature commander who didn't want to be there, had been a sure recipe for disaster.

Colonel Tho would gloat, his low opinion of Lieutenant Tam and the NPFF proven. Whatever he did about Lieutenant Tam, I knew I'd be in for an earful the next time he saw me. For the next couple of weeks, I managed to be busy and avoid his morning staff meetings.

I had a more pressing problem than enduring the province chief's derision; somehow I had to find a way to get the one-hundred-man NPFF company out of their barracks and into the war.

10

"YOU KNOW WHAT MY MEN CALL the National Police, don't you?" the American advisor, a major, attached to the South Vietnamese White Horse Squadron in Tam Ky asked. "They call them the White Mice."

I had been prepared for that, but I had to find a way for the National Police Field Force to gain experience and build some confidence. One way, I thought, was to pair them with American or Vietnamese military units

"After that farce with the keys to their truck the other morning, it's pretty clear that your police just don't want to fight," the major said. "I don't think my counterpart is going to want to risk something like that with the White Horse Squadron involved."

I had been searching for a mission for the NPFF for days, but the collapse of the operation against Viet Cong snipers hiding in a flood-bound hamlet along Route #1 before it even got underway and the province chief's ranting about it had made my search to find a Vietnamese or US unit willing to take them along on an operation seem futile. Worse, we were weeks into the rainy season, and everyone's mood seemed foul.

Mere weeks after Leroy Anderson stocked the new fish hatchery with smolt, the Vietnamese neighbors dropped hand grenades into the pond, scooping up the tiny fish that floated belly-up to the surface and frying them up for breakfast. Leroy was outraged. Colonel Tho had promised a fence or a guard but had delivered neither. The wrath of the gruff Norwegian professor for once quieted the blustery province chief who piped down even about the police.

In the evenings at the MACV club, over beer and the now obligatory crème de menthe, I tried to persuade visiting Regional and Popular Forces advisors that cooperating in joint operations was in our respective organizations' best interest.

"The Popular Forces are only engaged in static defense," a lieutenant told me.

"My district chief has no respect for the police," said a captain, an advisor to a Regional Force company.

The officers seemed interested only in grousing about having to drink up the club's immense overstock of crème de menthe.

"Next time, we're going to get rum," the lieutenant averred. "Colonel Isley likes rum and as senior advisor, he's going to get to choose."

"Naw!" replied the captain. "Isley's gonna be retired, and we're gonna be home before that shit's drunk up!"

It just might be that long before I get the NPFF into the field, I thought, sinking into the dour mood that seemed to have settled over the table.

At our weekly staff meetings, I earnestly pointed out that the NPFF was able and available to search hamlets and villages for VC and root out the VC infrastructure.

"We just need a US or Vietnamese military unit to cordon off the area to prevent the VC from escaping and protect the police from a VC and NVA counterattack while they're working in the hamlet or village," I pleaded. But after the "lost keys" incident, nobody seemed to want to work with the NPFF.

The weeks of inaction following the incident weighed on the morale of the police who found themselves the butt of jokes around Tam Ky. Further darkening their mood, one night, the VC attacked the barracks of the NPFF platoon assigned to a static defense post in the south end of town, causing mayhem among the sleeping police but no serious injuries. The next day, with conjured-up bravado, the police told exaggerated tales of driving off the VC. But none had been captured, no bodies found, nor were there trails of blood indicating that a lifeless or seriously injured VC had been dragged off by his comrades. The hapless police were left empty-handed with nothing they could show to count coup against the Viet Cong.

Then one afternoon in November, an American major came to my office. He introduced himself as the operations officer for the Third Battalion of the Twenty-First Infantry, operating in the Que Son Valley west of Tam Ky. The Third/Twenty-First was engaged in hard-slogging infantry work rooting out North Vietnamese and hardcore VC units that had operated in the area for four years.

"I understand you are looking for missions for your police," the major said.

"That's right," I said.

"We've got a lot of rice farmers who, despite the fighting, remain in sparsely populated hamlets in my battalion's area of operations," the major said. "With no government protection, the peasants do the bidding of the VC who confiscate the bulk of the farmers' rice to feed themselves and the large North Vietnamese units operating in the Que Son Valley. We need help to identify and capture Viet Cong working among the villagers."

Good enough, I thought. Operating with an infantry unit engaged in search and destroy operations was outside the mission of civilian police, but as long as the NPFF was used to search for and identify VC fighters and their support cadres in the hamlets, this could work. In any case, it was as likely an opportunity to get the NPFF in action as I was going to get.

"I think I can get my counterpart, the province police chief, Captain Ha, to support this," I told the major after listening some more. I decided to bypass Lieutenant Tam from the outset. "But the NPFF company lacks the field gear necessary for an extended operation in the field. Can you help us on that?"

The major said the Third/Twenty-First would provide tents for the police and haul their rations from Tam Ky. We agreed that a single platoon, thirty men, would be rotated every two weeks. I escorted the major to Captain Ha's office.

Captain Ha readily agreed and sent for Lieutenant Tam. When the major and I explained the operation to the NPFF commander, Lieutenant Tam, realizing that Captain Ha had already assented, squirmed like a worm about to be impaled on a fishhook. For the idle combat police, it was finally to be boots and saddles.

Knowing that the operation, deep in contested territory, would be sink or swim for the NPFF platoon and they would need a motivated leader, I convinced Lieutenant Tam that as company commander his presence was needed in Tam Ky. To his credit, he selected Redactor Nguyen Tu, a tall, earnest young officer, who was competent and respected by his men, to lead the platoon to be deployed with the Third/Twenty-First.

The following afternoon, four Huey gunships shuttled the NPFF platoon and me to Landing Zone Center, the operations base of the Third/Twenty-First. The heavily fortified encampment was sited on a mountaintop surrounded by jungle near the village of Nui Loc Son. The first flight had to stand off because the US troops on the defense perimeter had enemy troops in contact. When the firing stopped and we sat down, the NPFF were escorted to their bivouac area while I met with battalion staff and rifle company commanders to discuss how the police would be utilized.

"We realize many of the VC are going to escape, but we're operating in very difficult terrain, mountainous, thick jungle," the rifle company commanders not unexpectedly argued when I explained the cordon and search operation favored by the NPFF. "It would be nearly impossible for us to throw up a cordon around a hamlet before the police go in. We need the police to screen the villagers and help us develop intelligence."

Success in the pacification war called for the abandonment of the search and destroy tactic theretofore employed by US units with the goal of forcing peasants in Communist-controlled areas to relocate to hamlets that could be protected by the South Vietnamese government. The new strategy, which made a lot more sense to me, called for clearing the VC out of such areas and helping the local population organize self-defense forces. Key to the plan was President Thieu's decision to arm the villagers, a measure his critics in the American press had said he would never undertake. Supplanting the search and destroy tactic, the police would enter a pacified village or hamlet and search out the VC and their infrastructure while a South Vietnamese or US infantry unit blocked escape and prevented a VC counterattack.

I wasn't going to get that here, as NVA forces dominated the area, but at least the police would be interacting with the peasants in the hamlets and gain experience working with a US military unit. The NPFF would no longer languish in a static defense role in Tam Ky by default. It was not optimum, but I'd have to go along with the opportunity the US unit offered.

I stuck around Landing Zone Center for two days, ironing out kinks and ensuring myself that the platoon would not merely be used as cannon fodder. The police were upbeat, the Americans glad to have them. I grew confident of Redactor Tu and the support of the US unit. Sensing the operation would succeed without further help from me, I returned to Tam Ky.

My confidence turned out to be well placed. Despite being armed only with light, semi-automatic carbines, the platoon, accounted for three VC killed and five captured. Two of the NPFF were wounded during operations and medevacked to the US field hospital in Chu Lai. Both were back in Tam Ky within days. At the end of two weeks, the platoon returned to town full of war stories and brimming with newfound confidence. The next platoon in line to go to Nui Loc Son boarded the choppers eagerly.

Even Colonel Tho was impressed, and the next morning in his staff meeting, he spoke the first words of praise for the NPFF that I had heard him utter. I wrote a letter of commendation for Redactor Tu that was published in the police gazette that month. Brimming with pride and relief, that night I bought the bar at the MACV club.

But both Captain Ha and I had known from the start that infantry search and destroy operations were outside the parameters for deployment of the NPFF, and if the mission was misportrayed in Saigon, the operation would be doomed. It was soon to come.

Lieutenant Tam chose to lead the third deployment to Nui Loc Son himself and after just a few days demanded that the NPFF be withdrawn. The NPFF were being used as infantry, not police, he complained.

Technically, he had a point, but still the police were working in populated areas, identifying, capturing, or killing VC and rooting out their infrastructure. That was their mission. In my view, the joint operation was a success, and it had done wonders for the unit's competence and morale. I ignored Lieutenant Tam's demand, but his complaints soon reached Saigon and were relayed back down the chain of command to Captain Ha.

"Mr. Harpold, the directorate general of National Police in Saigon says the police must be withdrawn from the operation in Nui Loc Son," Captain Ha said.

"We've made a commitment to the American unit that we must keep," I protested. "If we go back on our promise, we will lose face, and that will hurt the National Police Field Force and us."

That seemed to be good enough for Captain Ha. He shrugged and left my office.

The police platoon had only a few days left in Nui Loc Son, and I let them stay. It was the height of the winter monsoon, and I knew the men would be wet and muddy. But the Saigon-bred Lieutenant Tam would be miserable. I knew also it was the end of all future such operations with the Third/Twenty-First. Nonetheless, I was satisfied and pleased that the NPFF company had turned a corner, but I'd have to be circumspect in lining up joint operations with American infantry units in the future.

11

"Đả đảo *Hồ Chí Minh!* Đả đảo *Hồ Chí Minh!*" Shouting in unison, pumping their right fists into the air, gaunt men in light-colored, pajama-like uniforms jumped to their feet as Mr. Dang ushered me into the crowded cell. Down with Ho Chi Minh, I thought they were chanting, but I asked the prison chief, to be sure.

Arrayed around concrete platforms that served for sleeping and sitting, the coerced ritual complete, the men stood silent and expressionless. There appeared to be more than a hundred prisoners in the confined space. The room was bare of furnishings or decoration. Barred, unglazed windows set high in the unpainted masonry walls allowed in little light and air.

The regimentation, the starkness must be what a Soviet gulag is like, I thought. But this was South Vietnam, a US ally, and I was the prison chief's American advisor. The enormity of my professional and moral responsibility swept over me.

I had no background or training in penology. *What are the standards*, I asked, *those of the Western world or of the East?* I knew little about the former and nothing of the latter, and I had little guidance from USAID. I was flying by the seat of my pants and decided I would be best guided by my conscience.

"The prisoners are fed twice a day," Mr. Dang volunteered. I nodded, getting that he wanted me to understand that. I wondered if the prisoners were allowed outside to exercise.

The fortress-like prison was built around a central courtyard, itself crowded with service structures. In cells in two more wings, I experienced a repeat of the first, hollow-eyed men leaping to their feet as we entered, denouncing Ho Chi Minh.

Not quite unexpectedly, the fourth wing held women, but my heart leapt into my throat when I saw that many of them held babies or clutched the hands of small children.

"They are the wives of Viet Cong," Mr. Dang explained. "They are VC, too. In Vietnam, we do not separate children from their mothers."

"How about the men? How many are serving criminal sentences?" I asked when we got back to Mr. Dang's office.

"All are Viet Cong or North Vietnamese soldiers," Dang said, looking surprised that I should ask such a question. "They have been tried by a military tribunal." In my short time in Tam Ky, I had learned that seemingly there were no criminals; all crime was blamed on the VC. The men were internees, I realized, with no hope of release until somehow, someway, the war was resolved.

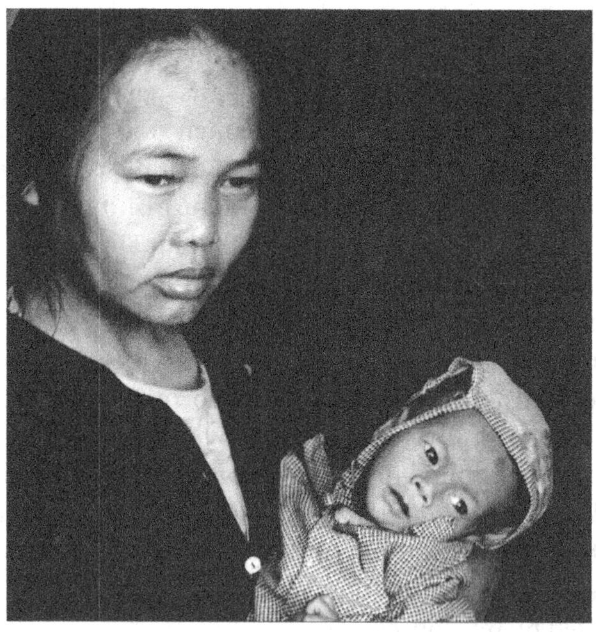

Bà Duong Thi Can and her three-month-old child, detained by US troops and sentenced by a South Vietnamese military tribunal as a Viet Cong sympathizer to an indeterminate confinement in the Quang Tin Provincial prison. Bà Can made her child's clothing on a sewing machine donated to the prison by the Mennonite Central Committee, which also provided sewing lessons and donated canned milk for the infants. Photo courtesy of Doug Hostetter.

That night over beer at the MACV club, I shared my experience that day with Dave Glennon, and Dr. Glenn Connors, a US Navy doctor who worked at the province hospital. Both men, on and off duty, devoted their skills and tireless energy to treating Vietnamese civilians.

"Prisoners confined in such close quarters are bound to have TB," Dave said. "The place is probably a breeding ground for it," Dr. Connors agreed.

The next day, I arranged with Mr. Dang for the two doctors to go inside the prison and take a look. In the days following, they administered TB tests to all four hundred inmates.

"Almost all have TB," Dr. Connors reported when the tests had been read, and we huddled over what to do about it. "As a practical matter, since there is very little the prisoners do in the facility other than sleep, they should probably just be treated in place."

Dave was able to get medicine from USAID. We had talked about the inevitability of at least a portion of it being diverted to the black market, and as often as they could, Dave or Dr. Connors monitored its delivery to the patients. I was able to get program funds for the in-country purchase of concrete and lumber to build an infirmary, and we persuaded the US Navy Construction Battalion (Seabee) detachment billeted in Tam Ky to build it.

I spent as much time as I could with Mr. Dang, learning about the Vietnamese penal system from him and, in the course of it, building a rapport so we could work together. We talked about ways to improve the prisoner's diet.

"We can plant a garden and grow vegetables if Colonel Tho will permit us to use the land outside the prison walls, but we'll need seed," Mr. Dang proposed. The province chief readily assented. Agriculture advisor, Leroy Anderson, obtained seed from USAID and pitched in with advice and supervision.

I persuaded Mr. Dang to move most of the support activities outside the prison walls, including the thatch house he and his family occupied, clearing the way for an exercise yard and a children's playground. We had no play equipment, but it didn't seem to matter. The kids got fresh air and sunlight. The prison yard got the joyful sound of children at play.

Then one afternoon, as if guided to me by a Divine hand, two young missionaries who worked for Vietnam Christian Service, Doug Hostetter and Maurice Byrne, came to my office. I had seen the pair around Tam Ky riding double on their Vespa motor scooter. They did not seem to associate much with other Americans but often sought Dave Glennon to treat sick or wounded Vietnamese civilians.

"We'd like to start a literacy program in the prison and sewing classes for the women," the two missionaries said. "The Mennonite Church in America is sending us twenty treadle sewing machines for the project."

I took Doug and Maurice to meet Mr. Dang. He was dubious and non-committal. The two missionaries were pacifists and were rumored to have VC friends and stand with their backs turned when American convoys passed through town. The flag could bear that, I thought, and, like most of the USAID advisors, I admired them for living their convictions, but I was privately worried it would be an issue with the province chief. I decided to broach it head on.

Colonel Tho was often brusque and prone to bully subordinates. On the other hand, privately, I had found an easy rapport with the province chief, discovering at our introductory meeting that we both were the fathers of three daughters but no sons. In a society that treasured sons by naming them for flowers but only numbered girls, it brought both of us unwanted pity. We compared notes about our daughters often, and Colonel Tho seemed to appreciate the opportunity.

I thought if I could get the matter of literacy classes in the prison to Colonel Tho in a private setting, at a place and time he didn't have an audience, Doug and Maurice stood a chance.

"What does their religion say to do when we're attacked by an enemy who slays our women and children?" Colonel Tho challenged.

"They're Christians," I said. "The Mennonites are humanitarians. They simply want to teach children and illiterate adults in the prison how to read and write and the women how to sew." I reminded the province chief of the bit of news we both had just received; The International Committee of the Red Cross was planning to inspect the prison in less than two months' time. "The sewing and literacy classes the Mennonites are prepared to provide will help present the prison in the best possible light," I said.

A few days later, Mr. Dang came to my office to tell me Colonel Tho had approved. Doug and Maurice were pleased. Having been shocked by the evidence of malnutrition among the children, they began immediately to deliver stocks of canned milk to the prison.

The ever-helpful Seabees built wooden bench desks for the children. The American Red Cross representative in Tam Ky gave me several cases of school supplies donated by elementary school children in California for refugee children. As a classroom project, the students had packed individual cartons with a small box of crayons, pads of colored notepaper, a small coloring book, a pencil and sharpener, an eraser, stickers, and a small plastic toy.

The teachers sent along letters with the boxes, asking to know about the children who received the gifts. I struggled over how to respond. The Vietnamese children had literally nothing in material goods, and they treasured these small items, but I worried about telling first and second grade students that these children were in a prison. My daughters were that age, perhaps even participating in similar drives at Noble Elementary School in Bakersfield. I wrote home and asked Dominica what she thought.

"The girls would be anguished, as am I," Dominica replied. "I don't think you ought to mention it."

I wrote to the teachers and told them that the children had been forced from their homes by war, as indeed they were, and told them about Doug and Maurice's literacy project without mentioning the prison.

A few days before the inspection team from Geneva arrived, I went to the prison to check on progress. The problem of overcrowding would not soon be resolved, I knew. The facility was built to house 180 detainees, but actually held more. Still, I thought we could show progress. The prisoners were being rotated through the exercise yard, providing each an hour a day of fresh air and sunlight. The garden was already producing vegetables. The prison was raising pigs for slaughter, fed by USAID bulgur wheat sent to Vietnam to feed starving people but which was not part of the Vietnamese diet. The sewing and literacy classes set up by Doug and Maurice had become a showpiece and a source of pride for Colonel Tho and Mr. Dang.

We were doing what we could about the tuberculosis epidemic—at least we were diagnosing prisoners with the disease and giving them medicine. But I was stunned to find that Mr. Dang had moved his family into the recently completed infirmary.

"You've got to get out of there!" I yelled. "If the Red Cross inspectors see this, they'll believe our efforts are insincere, and we'll get credit for nothing! We'll lose face!"

"My family and I have no place else to live," Mr. Dang pleaded. "We moved to make way for the children's playground."

"Okay," I said, chastened. He had not protested at the time, probably out of deference to me, I thought sheepishly. "You have to move out, now. Find some temporary place in town. When the inspectors are gone, I'll ask the Seabees to build new quarters for you and your family."

Wanting to showcase Mr. Dang and Colonel Tho for their improvements at the prison, I did not meet the Red Cross officials on their arrival in Tam Ky. That would be their responsibility. Instead, I went to the prison knowing the inspection would be underway. I found Mr. Dang and the three Swiss officials in the dispensary.

On each of the six beds lay a grinning "patient," who was obviously too healthy to be a prisoner. I recognized a couple of them as guards. Mr. Dang had turned the inspection into a burlesque! Chagrinned, I sighed and stayed in the background while, through an interpreter, he gave meandering, often evasive, answers to the inspection team's probing questions.

The cells had been freshly cleaned, the prisoners well rehearsed, their clothing and bodies freshly washed, but not even the perfectly adequate meal of rice, chicken, and initial harvest of the prison's home-grown vegetables could soften their sallow, expressionless faces. Only when we arrived at the women's wing did the Swiss inspector's demeanor seem to briefly brighten. Women worked at the sewing machines. Children sat at the bench desks made for them by the Seabees, absorbed in their coloring books and crayons from the American schoolchildren.

I cringed again when at noontime we returned to the dispensary. Mr. Dang had sent away the "patients," cleared away the beds, and set up a table for lunch. I took the chair next to the head of the inspection team, an avuncular Swiss official in late middle age. Mr. Dang sat across from us. He appeared under pressure, and I felt a little sorry for him. One of the inspectors passed him a form to sign, but as if for his closing act, he put a pair of half-frame glasses on his nose upside down, drawing bemused looks from the Swiss.

The Red Cross officials and I made small talk as we ate. My thoughts returned to my first impression of the prison, a gulag, at best a warehouse for four hundred captive men and women. The progress Doug, Maurice, Dave, and Dr. Connors, even Mr. Dang and Colonel Tho, had made seemed minuscule. Dejected, I nevertheless gently probed the Swiss for some reaction, but the leader parried by saying we would receive their report in writing "in a fortnight."

"We're trying through these inspections to bring about improvements for detainees and host countries alike," he said.

Perhaps as a bone, he added, "When Americans are involved, conditions are better."

12

TET 1969, THE FIRST DAY OF THE LUNAR NEW YEAR, dawned sunny and warm, and I lingered in bed watching the day grow brighter through cracks in the shutters. A knock came at my door. Half-dressed, I pulled it open. Standing in the hallway, hand raised to his eyebrow in a salute, his round face split by a big grin, was Hau, the chief of our Nung guard force.

I was puzzled. Chief Hau had never appeared at my room before, choosing to conduct his business with me outside in the compound or while we crouched side by side in the sandbag bunker at the top of the front wall during alerts, peering beyond the reach of our perimeter lights into the pitch-black savannah that stretched to the west. Then it dawned on me. This was a social call, customary on the first morning of Tết.

I was planning on making a number of visits myself later in the morning, but not expecting anyone to come to my room, I had none of the foods that tradition required be served on such a visit. Nor did I have a gift for Hau. Nevertheless, I invited him in, offering him my desk chair while I opened a new bottle of Johnny Walker Red. I poured each of us a generous amount of the Scotch and perched on the edge of my bed.

"*An khang thịnh vượng*" (security, good health, prosperity), I toasted in Vietnamese, lifting my glass. I wondered if he understood.

"Hop-py Neu Yar," Hau managed, the only English words I had ever heard him attempt. We grinned at each other and sipped the amber liquor neat.

Absently, I mused if Hau was lucky or not. According to tradition, the first person to cross the threshold on the morning of Tet determines the host family's luck for the remainder of the year, and householders go to elaborate lengths to make sure he or she is known for good fortune. I suspected that Hau considered me lucky, but I could only guess if he was or not. I was surprised to discover it seemed to matter to me. Did it reflect a fear for my safety? Insecurity over my effectiveness as an advisor? While we sipped the Scotch, I strove to contain my misgivings.

When he had drained his glass, still grinning, his face flushed from the alcohol, Chief Hau stood and saluted. Still abashed at not having anticipated his visit, I gave him the rest of the bottle to share with his men. The previous afternoon, I had given him and each of his men a red envelope stuffed with piastres—USAID gave their Vietnamese employees an extra month's pay at Tet–and I hoped it would cover for my loutishness in not having prepared for his visit.

At ten a.m., as planned, Deputy Chief of Police Thieu arrived to escort me to the homes of other police commanders and important local officials. We went to his house first, and I was welcomed by his wife and children. Mr. Thieu opened a fresh bottle of Martell cognac while his wife served the traditional Tet foods in turn: a carrot, an onion, a piece of pork, and a rice cake.

From left to right: Mr. Ban, the author, and Mr. So celebrate Tet at Mr. Ban's house.

Then it was off to Mr. Ban's house, the chief of the Resource Control police, followed by a stop at Mr. Nghia's, the chief of the Special Branch police. We picked up an entourage that seemed to grow at each stop.

"To be given the first and last drink from a bottle at Tết is a very great honor and will bring you very good fortune in the New Year," Mr. Thieu assured me at a stop later in the morning as our host drained the last of a bottle of cognac into my glass. Not many minutes earlier, he had poured me the first drink from the freshly opened bottle before passing it to the rest of the revelers, including those who now spilled out of the small house into the front yard.

By two p.m., I was past my limit and asked to be taken back to my quarters. Mr. Thieu was effusively apologetic, but as we had still more visits to make, he asked if he could return later. I offered equally gracious thanks and apologies but declined. I spent the rest of the day and into the night sleeping it off.

* * *

I had not found the Vietnamese indifferent or resentful, as often depicted in the American press reports peddled to the public back home. Instead, I enjoyed working with my Vietnamese counterparts, and until now, I had worried if they liked me. But from my arrival the previous fall, they had treated me graciously.

The welcoming dinner thrown for me by Captain Ha in September had seemed to set a tone, and he continued to be a generous host. At Christmas, his wife gave me a beautiful silk ao dai and lacquered, high-heeled shoes to send to my wife. On a trip to a conference in Danang, he had hosted me lavishly, well beyond what I suspected he could afford on an army captain's pay.

"Mr. Harpold. You go to Danang. Fok around. I kill you die," my secretary, Bà Mui, warned me with palpable disgust when I had told her of the impending trip with Captain Ha. I didn't learn until after he was transferred, shortly after Christmas, that in addition to his position as province chief of police, Captain Ha was the bagman for the brothels that served South Vietnamese soldiers in and around Tam Ky.

My Vietnamese counterparts displayed their acceptance of me in other ways, too. Around Tam Ky, I wore a small revolver on my belt in a cross-draw holster. I didn't realize the attention it drew until I saw one day that the uniformed police officers who stood on steel-drum pedestals directing traffic at the town's main intersections also were wearing their .38s on their left hip, the butt of the gun jutting forward under the flap of their leather holster.

The South Vietnamese officers who frequented province headquarters picked up the style. Even Colonel Tho caught the bug, and at a morning staff meeting, I noticed him wearing his .45, butt forward, on his left hip.

I was mildly flattered by the imitation until the next issue of a law enforcement journal from the States arrived. It carried an article pointing out that 70 percent of all officers who were shot by their own gun had been wearing their weapon cross-draw style. Wearing the gun on the left hip required a right-handed officer to reach across his body, a maneuver easily blocked by an assailant grappling the officer from the front. Cautioned, I began wearing my revolver on my right hip, and the cross-draw fad soon ended.

There was nothing to be done about the sideburn fad, however, except to smile. I wore flared muttonchops that, despite their lack of facial hair, young Vietnamese men tried to imitate by letting strands of head-hair dangle down the side of their face in front of their ears.

My circle of acquaintances in Tam Ky had grown large, and I was often asked if I could get clothing for them from the States. I wore broadcloth tattersall shirts and green or tan Wrangler jeans, attire much envied by young Vietnamese. But the cost of the items, although modest in the United States, was frequently well beyond their means, leading to embarrassment and loss of face. I thought about simply giving the sought-after item as a gift, but doing it for just one and not for all was out of the question. Reluctantly, I settled on a policy of not offering to.

I made an exception for Mui, who had just had a baby. My wife sent over a JC Penny catalog that I gave her and asked that she choose something for herself and her infant. The next day, she brought it back.

"Mr. Harpold, you take this away," she said, dropping the catalog on my desk. "I look at this and get too confused. You get for me one bathrobe and one pair of shoes for my baby."

Dominica sent over a quilted, nylon robe for Mui and a pair of red shoes with white, bunny-rabbit ears for her baby.

* * *

The Year of the Rooster did not dawn well for my interpreter, Hoang. He and Cô Hai thought the year to be auspicious for their marriage, which required a family negotiation. Over Tet, Hoang brought his father down from Quang Tri. Hoang purchased many gifts for Hai's family, and I flew Hoang, his father, Cô Hai, and the gifts to Tien Phuoc in the four-seat Helio Courier I regularly chartered from Air America.

But the marriage negotiation did not go well. Despite the gifts, Hoang's very generous USAID salary, and the power signified by the arrival of Hoang and his father in Tien Phuoc in the silver aircraft, Cô Hai's family set a wedding date one year off. It was the bride's family's way of saying they did not approve of the marriage. Hoang and Cô Hai were devastated.

I had thought they had everything going for them—youth, beauty, and dreams—and I felt bad for the young couple who remained devoted to each other. But their future, dictated by family and tradition, was beyond their control. They did not give up. I admired them for that, but I found myself wondering what chance they and their offspring would have in a nation whose fortunes at that juncture of the war were still very much in doubt.

* * *

There had been changes in the few months since my arrival. The immature Lieutenant Tam was gone, replaced by another scion of a Saigon family but one willing to try. Because of the success of the National Police Field Force operations with the Third/Twenty-First and other US and South Vietnamese units, a second, experienced, NPFF company of one hundred men was transferred to the province from service near the Demilitarized Zone.

Thanks to the help of my fellow USAID advisors and the two young, Vietnam Christian Service missionaries, I had a modest program of improvement going in the prison. Affable, but ineffective, Captain Ha had been transferred back to the army. A young police professional, Nguyen An Vinh, was slated to replace him as province national police chief. Under USAID sponsorship, Vinh had spent a year studying police management at Michigan State University. I looked forward to his arrival.

I had found frustrations and often feared for my safety in Tam Ky, fears shared by everyone in the community. Still, I had had a good start, I thought, and I was looking forward to my remaining year and a half in Vietnam.

In other circumstances, I would not have troubled myself about whether my first visitor the morning of the first day of Tết, the Nung guard captain, Hua, was a fortunate man, but now I did. I had been in the country long enough to know that, as often as not, things were not as they seemed, what was wished often did not happen, and good luck often came in handy.

Rice planting would soon begin in the paddies around Tam Ky, and now I as well as the Vietnamese yearned for good fortune in 1969, the Year of the Rooster.

13

THE CLOTH CURTAINS THAT DECORATED the windows of the single-story, wood-framed building were unusual enough, but the white linen tablecloths and freshly cut flowers arranged in small, cut-glass vases that graced each table especially drew my attention. Heavy silver salad and dinner forks rested at the left of each place setting; a table knife, teaspoon, soupspoon, and fish fork on the right. Peeled shrimp arrayed on a bed of crushed ice in a stemmed glass bowl set on a white service plate awaited each diner. I could have just entered the dining room of the St. Francis, the settings were so perfect, but San Francisco was half a world and a good chunk of my life away.

My genial host, Fred Hunt, ushered me to a table. My jaw agape at the unexpected elegance, I pulled out a chair, a sturdy bentwood, I noted, not the flimsy, war-weary variety that graced the few cafés in Tam Ky.

"I have to take care of something in the kitchen," Fred explained. "I'll be right back." He wore a white, short-sleeve shirt loose over his considerable girth. His fleshy jowls and short-cropped blond hair looked par for a professional chef. As he turned, his lively blue eyes took in every detail of his guests and their needs. Having met Fred only minutes before, I had to remind myself that he was the USAID Public Safety advisor in Hoi An and the retired sheriff of Fresno County, California.

My throat tasted of dust from the mostly unpaved road, and I reached for one of the two crystal goblets that sat at the top of my plate. I filled it from a pitcher of iced tea, the silver sides glistening with condensation. A plump Vietnamese woman wearing a hair net and a white apron appeared at my shoulder with a tray of hot towels, selecting one with a pair of chopsticks and passing it to me. I buried my face in the warm, moist folds, wiping away the red-clay dust of the road that caked my face and neck. I finished by scrubbing my wrists and hands.

I had driven the forty miles up to Hoi An at the request of Fred's counterpart, the chief of the National Police of Quang Nam Province. The young female secretaries who worked in the police headquarters in Hoi An were complaining about Fred's misuse of Vietnamese language, and the chief felt it was too delicate a matter for him to be able to talk to Fred himself. He called my counterpart in Tam Ky, Chief Vinh, who suggested I could help.

During my orientation in Saigon, I had heard rumors of Fred's dining room. I envisioned a character in a Joseph Conrad story, an Englishman deep in the interior of Africa dressing for dinner and directing his servants as he had in his Victorian homeland. The American equivalent of British Raj had come to Vietnam, I mused as I waited for Fred's return. I thought of other USAID advisers in headquarters jobs in Saigon and Danang who made themselves too comfortable, often taking Vietnamese concubines. The ugly Americans, I had sneered, but I hoped Fred wasn't one of them.

I felt the extra months of Vietnamese language and culture classes I had received at the Foreign Service Institute prepared me to work with the police in rural Vietnam better than could the older, more experienced men who had come from police departments in big US cities and had been given little or no language training. The need for my visit to Hoi An was proof of the point, I thought, smugly.

"Mike, this is Colonel Nguyen, the province chief," Fred said, arriving back from the kitchen. I partially rose and stuck my hand out to the Vietnamese officer who seated himself next to me.

"How do you do?" the province chief said, appraising my brown and beige National Police Field Force cammies. "I see you are a police adviser; I hope you are not here to replace Mr. Hunt?"

"No, Colonel," I assured him. "This is a purely social visit. A chance to eat at Mr. Hunt's table."

"Yes," the colonel replied. "Mr. Hunt has a very good reputation for hospitality. He is a very effective advisor."

The dining room filled with an assortment of American and Vietnamese officials. Fred introduced a slender, balding man, a surgeon from Chicago, who worked in the province hospital. The fourth diner at our table was a Red Cross worker from Oregon who helped resettle refugees.

A waitress served a green salad. I looked at Fred.

"It's okay, Mike," he said, reading my expression. Starved for fresh lettuce, when I finished, I asked for seconds. For the main course, a waitress ladled Hungarian goulash into our bowls, tender cubes of beef nestled amidst green peppers and chunks of tomatoes in a thick brown sauce seasoned with garlic and paprika.

"How do you do this, Fred?" I asked. "Where do you get this stuff?"

"Well, cooking is my hobby, particularly French cooking," Fred replied. "I've got Americans who come all the way down from Danang just to eat here, and they bring stuff: a crate of lettuce, a case of frozen steaks, all sorts of things. The spices and seafood I can generally get in the local market. The French did a great job teaching the Vietnamese how to cook, and you'd be amazed to see how much stuff from France is still available. I bring my counterpart here all the time, sometimes his family too. He loves it."

After lunch was cleared away, I followed Fred to the National Police headquarters. Save for a sole policeman who drowsed at a desk by the front door, the Asian-style stucco building was deserted for the noon siesta. I had been waiting until we got to Fred's office before bringing up my business, but he steered me instead into his counterpart's office.

"Look at this, Mike," he said, pulling back a curtain and revealing a whiteboard covered with bar charts. "These graphs show the training progress of every section in the organization, the National Police Field Force, Special Branch, admin, everybody. This chart shows where we are training the teams for the new National Identity Card program." A line graph indicated that training for the project was close to completion.

"My God, Fred," I stammered, "I don't think we've even started."

Kick-off date for the nationwide implementation of the new ID card was just weeks away, and in Tam Ky, I was worried. Teams had to be recruited and trained before being sent out to district towns and villages to fingerprint and photograph the populace for the new ID. I had no idea where preparations stood or if Chief Vinh had even started. The project was a top national priority and had a sixty-day window for completion. The cameras and equipment had arrived in Tam Ky, but despite my nagging, I had gotten little in the way of a progress report from Vinh.

"I wish I could get an organized training program going in Tam Ky," I ruminated. "Even when one of my NPFF companies got their new M-16s last month, I couldn't get them to do any kind of organized training. They say there's a war on and they don't have time."

"I've heard that a few times," the older man sympathized. "Mike, you've probably heard this already, but you've got to remember that these little guys have been fighting this war for over ten years and may still be fighting it when we're gone. Your chief wants to know what you bring to the game," Fred continued. "You may have to come up with something he wants before he'll listen to you, and sometimes his needs aren't readily apparent.

"Take my dining room, for instance. We're not far from Danang, and bigwigs come down here all the time. My counterpart can't afford to entertain them; that's why he likes to come to my dining room. I encourage him to invite anyone he wants, the province chief—you met him there today—the headquarters honchos, even local political leaders. I let him act like that dining room is his own. It makes him look good, and he's grateful. In turn he does the things he knows are important to me."

I had a lot to think about as we walked across the hall to Fred's office, but there was little time for reflection. I had my business to take care of and get back to Tam Ky before Route #1 was barricaded for the night.

"Fred," I started when we were seated at his desk, "my counterpart, Chief Vinh, asked me to come up here today."

The big man shot me a quizzical look.

"Your counterpart called him and said that every morning when you come into headquarters here, you grab the Vietnamese secretaries in a bear hug and say, 'Grr-rr, I'm the big *khăn khó*!'"

Fred looked defensive. "Yeah, I do that. You know how cute these little girls are, dressed so neat in their pretty ao dais and everything. I'm just being friendly, Mike. I grab ''em and tell them I'm the big tiger. They always giggle."

"Everyone realizes you're trying to be friendly, Fred." I shifted on my chair. "But what you're actually saying is 'Grr-rr , I'm the big prick!'"

Taken aback, the large man shifted in his chair, then leaned forward, elbows on his knees, and examined his hands. "Mike, that's not what I mean—I don't mean that."

"I know, Fred. You think you're saying tiger, but you're missing the tone. The word for tiger is *con hổ*. Try this: *con*, short *o*, then *hổ* with an inflexion."

"Can bo," he stammered, missing the vital tones. "Aw, Mike. I can't do this. I've made a fool of myself. I'll stop; I'll just not do it again. I can't do this stuff."

"Don't worry about it, Fred," I offered sympathetically.

"I do worry about it, Mike. I care an awful lot what these people think of me. How am I going to look my counterpart in the eye after this? No wonder he wasn't at the table today."

"Fred, I think your counterpart cares an awful lot about how his staff thinks of you, too. There were many other ways he could have handled this, including simply letting you go on making a fool of yourself, but he didn't."

"But why couldn't he just come out and tell me himself?"

"He thinks too much of you, Fred. He couldn't risk offending you. He doesn't want you to lose face. If you lose face, so does he, and he doesn't want that."

"You won't tell anyone else about this, will you, Mike?" He paused a long time and added, "The guys up in Danang?"

"No, Fred. It's between you and me."

Not wanting to be on the road after dark, I had to hurry on the long drive back to Tam Ky, but I didn't worry too much about Fred. Instead, I thought about the training charts on his counterpart's wall and pondered what I could do to encourage Chief Vinh to do the same when I got back. I pondered what among my talents Vinh could find useful and how I could build on that to get him to do what was important to me. How could I become as successful an advisor as Fred Hunt?

It seemed there had been lessons for both of us that day.

14

"THAT'S OUR OBJECTIVE," THE YOUNG AMERICAN lieutenant pointed out, handing me his binoculars. In early morning sunshine, we rode atop a boxy, tracked vehicle that could carry thirteen infantrymen in its interior and mounted two M60 machine guns and a .50-caliber machine gun on the top. From our vantage point, I could see a cluster of thatch houses nestled in a palm grove among the sandhills ahead of us. About three hundred yards from the hamlet, the dozen other armored cavalry assault vehicles behind us fanned out in a broad line and pulled abreast of us.

Without warning, the .50-caliber machine guns opened up, creating a fierce din. Redactor Thanh and his platoon of National Police Field Force bailed off the vehicles and took prone defensive positions, but the American troops, most of whom, like the lieutenant and me, were riding on top of the assault vehicles, remained in place. Puzzled, I looked for fire from the hamlet but could detect none.

"Why are you firing?" I yelled to the lieutenant over the din of the guns.

"We're reconnoitering by fire," the American officer yelled back. Through the binoculars, I could see peasants frantically scrambling to reach a partially buried, earthen and timber bunker at the edge of the hamlet.

"I don't see return fire," I yelled.

The lieutenant shrugged and worked his radio. The firing ceased, and the assault vehicles crawled closer to the hamlet, stopping at the tree line. I grabbed my .12-gauge shotgun and jumped down.

Apparently alerted by the lieutenant that I was unhappy about the .50-cal fire, the troop commander, a captain much older than I was, bustled over.

"After the NVA attacked us yesterday, we're not taking any chances," he declared. "They had to have come out of this village." It was not unusual for troops in combat to fire into a suspicious jungle thicket to preempt a possible ambush, but the assault vehicles had fired indiscriminately into a populated hamlet.

The previous afternoon, as the cavalry troop had proceeded single file through a ravine, North Vietnamese soldiers had ambushed the assault vehicles with rocket-propelled grenades and AK-47 fire. The platoon of NPFF had been riding exposed on top of the vehicles, and Redactor Thanh and the police had leapt off and charged up the steep banks. The North Vietnamese had been driven off, but two of the police had been killed and four others medevacked to the US hospital at Chu Lai. No Americans had been hurt.

I learned of their casualties that night when the bodies of the two slain policemen were flown back to Tam Ky. The platoon was part of a seasoned company of NPFF recently deployed to Tam Ky from the Demilitarized Zone. I was not surprised to learn of their heroism under fire, but the growing number of police casualties alarmed me.

Just weeks earlier, the platoon of National Police Field Force newly assigned to Tien Phuoc District had been ambushed by mortar fire while they stood in formation at a morning flag-raising ceremony in front of the district headquarters. Twelve men had been killed outright, including the platoon leader, Nguyen Tu, the earnest, young redactor who had led the platoon at the first of the successful joint operation with the US Third/Twenty-First Infantry at Nui Loc Son back in November. Twenty of his men were wounded; ten had suffered traumatic amputations. The thirty-man platoon had been virtually wiped out.

The platoon had formed up facing the flagpole in front of the district headquarters when in quick succession three mortar shells had exploded in their midst. Common sense dictated that a platoon of police, potentially vulnerable to indirect fire, not form up at a predictable time and place, and I troubled about why Redactor Tu had done so. Most likely, the platoon had been ordered by the district chief to stand reveille each morning, but in the aftermath of the tragedy, no one was saying.

Redactor Thanh, commander of the National Police Field Force company newly assigned to Tam Ky after service on the Demilitarized Zone, and the author.

I had yet to spend the night in Tien Phuoc and had known nothing of the platoon's morning formation. But an overnight visit would have revealed the hazardous practice and surely sparked greater involvement with the newly deployed police by the district chief and his US advisor, I told myself. The district chief's advisor, a US Army captain, said he didn't know how much he should have been involved with the police. As much as I hated the Viet Cong for the massacre of the men, I felt I had failed them, too.

Two weeks later, Redactor Thanh's platoon had departed Tam Ky with the troop of the US First/First Cavalry to sweep up the coast in territory the government did not control. Now they also had suffered casualties.

Early the following morning, Hoang and I choppered to the site of the operation. The captain commanding the cavalry troop was effusive in his praise of the police and credited their swift and courageous action, charging the attacking North Vietnamese soldiers, for saving his unit.

The Viet Cong and small North Vietnamese units were known to occupy the few populated hamlets in the target area, and the police were to be the search element in what I had been assured would be a classic cordon and search operation. According to the agreed-upon plan, the assault vehicles were to surround the hamlet, preventing escape while providing security for the police as they searched the hamlet for Viet Cong and North Vietnamese soldiers. But I had not anticipated the US unit would fire into the hamlet without first having received fire.

It was probable that the North Vietnamese unit that ambushed the cavalry troop was drawing support from the hamlet, I thought. Possibly they were even sheltering there, but enemy soldiers typically fled with the approach of a superior force. Firing into a populated hamlet, if we had not received fire from it, was not justified, but the captain was in charge of the operation and the safety of both of our contingents. I decided, for the moment at least, not to question it further.

Once in the hamlet, the police spread out along the narrow lanes between thatch houses. We encountered no armed resistance. I saw only women, children, and old people. Most were in a state of shock from the fusillade and eyed us fearfully. I broke off to find the log and earthen bunker I had seen from my position atop the assault vehicle.

The shelter was adjacent to the village well, and a crowd had gathered. At my approach, they broke into an agitated babble. An old man bled profusely from a shoulder wound, another from a head wound. A dazed old woman removed her hand from her mouth to show me the gaping, blood-filled hole where her teeth and tongue had been. The lieutenant and a radioman had followed me, and I turned to him.

"Are you going to patch these people up?" I asked archly.

"It's not up to me," he replied.

"All right," I answered evenly. "Ask the captain to come up on your radio."

Presently, the captain came on. I explained where I was and asked him to come over with a medic. He was not happy about it but soon appeared.

"These people need to be patched up," I said. There followed a long pause while the officer seemed to be evaluating me. Finally, he shook his head no.

"Captain, I have no authority over you, but I want you to fix these people up," I demanded.

"Awright!" he snapped, gesturing to his medics. "But, I ain't gonna medevac 'em."

After a few brusque instructions to the medics, the captain stalked off. Figuring I had gotten as much as I was going to get, I didn't push the captain further.

Methodically questioning the inhabitants as they went, the police searched through the thatch houses. A boy, a child of seven or eight, told them he knew where two soldiers were hiding and led a pair of policemen to a clearing. The lieutenant and I followed. Without warning, a sod hatch hidden by the tall grass popped open, and I caught a quick glimpse of two heads. One of the men threw a hand grenade at us before pulling the hatch closed. We dodged for cover, and it exploded harmlessly.

The police tried to persuade the men in the hole to surrender, but they did not respond. The wife of one of the men was found, and she in turn pleaded for her husband to come out. Finally, the lieutenant crawled to the hatch and rigged a quarter-pound block of plastique on top of it. The blast killed the men in the hole. The police pulled two bodies clad in North Vietnamese Army uniforms from it along with two AK-47s.

I pondered what would happen to the boy when we left and debated with Hoang and Redactor Thanh whether we should take him with us. The Vietnamese woman stood silently grieving over the body of her dead husband. Without warning, a Vietnamese soldier the American unit had brought along as an interpreter rushed up to the woman and shot her in the head. I stood just a few feet away, and in my peripheral vision, I saw her arms flail upward as she fell over backwards. I was stunned speechless. The lieutenant shrugged and walked away.

The Vietnamese soldier had been acting erratically all morning and seemed to be drunk or under the influence of drugs. The police shunned him, and Redactor Thanh had pointed him out as a potential problem. I had suggested to the captain that he use Hoang to talk to Redactor Thanh, but he shrugged off the offer. After the woman's murder, he did nothing to rebuke or restrain the soldier who from then on stayed out of view.

In the afternoon, the tracked vehicles continued north, paralleling the coast through a wooded area. The soldiers found fishing nets hidden in the tall grass and burned them. Redactor Thanh and his men did not join in. The mission at that point had reverted to search and destroy, designed to deprive the Viet Cong and North Vietnamese of sources of food and shelter and drive recalcitrant civilian populations into territory controlled by the South Vietnamese government. But, as in the Quezon valley where the police that fall had operated with US troops, villagers were attached to their ancestral lands and reluctant to leave, choosing to ride out depredations inflicted by both sides.

An infantryman reported by radio that he had found an old man concealed in the weeds, apparently hidden there by the villagers. He was too old and weak to get up and walk, and the soldier asked what to do.

I told the lieutenant I would send a couple of police, but he grabbed his M16 and jumped down from the assault vehicle. He looked me straight in the eye, a look I interpreted as either "Don't worry I'm not going to waste him" or "I'll take care of it, and you won't have to witness how." Choosing to believe the American officer would not kill a non-combatant, an old man, in cold blood, I did not follow.

A few moments later, a single shot rang out. Returning, the lieutenant climbed back to his seat, looked at me, and nodded. My heart in my throat, I couldn't ask what he had done. I pondered if he had wasted the old man or if he had meant to signal me that he had spared him, firing into the ground to save face with his men.

I was witnessing atrocities that I was powerless to prevent, yet morally I was obliged to. There was no justification for an armored unit not under attack to conduct a recon by fire against a civilian hamlet with their heavy automatic weapons. The officers exercised no control over their interpreter, and he had committed a murder. And, whether or not the lieutenant had actually shot the old man, it was not acceptable to maintain a command atmosphere that seemed to tolerate the taking of non-combatant lives.

At West Point, I had been taught that discipline guides a soldier in battle. Where none of the yardsticks of morality is present, he relies upon his training and the orders of his superiors. But the officers in this unit appeared characterized by indifference. I was convinced that the operation must end. The way to do that, I concluded, was to withdraw the police platoon.

I had no direct authority over Redactor Thanh, and he could not withdraw his men on his own. Chief Vinh could call them back, I decided, but I had no way to contact him. I had planned to spend several days in the field with the police and the cavalry troop, but I decided instead to return to Tam Ky. When we reached a night bivouac area and a Huey came in with supplies, Hoang and I took the opportunity to leave with it.

We got back to Tam Ky after dark, and I went directly to see Chief Vinh. We talked quietly on the darkened street in front of his house. I related what had occurred during the operation and came right to the point, asking Vinh to withdraw the police.

"How did the platoon perform?" Vinh asked.

"Admirably," I said. "On their own initiative, they charged the North Vietnamese ambushers, and the US captain credits them with having saved his men and their assault vehicles. The police did not join in firing on the hamlet and did not participate in the murders of the civilians. It was the police who located the North Vietnamese soldiers and tried to talk them out of the spider hole."

"The men in this company have fought in Quang Tri Province, at the Demilitarized Zone," Vinh said finally. "They are far more experienced than the young GIs who are rotated in and out and only stay in Vietnam for a year. The police are here all the time, always subject to attack by the enemy as we saw in Tien Phuoc. They hate the Viet Cong and the North Vietnamese just like the American soldiers who also are killed by booby traps and ambushes. But the police don't fear the Vietnamese people as the young Americans do. The soldiers' fear of the Vietnamese people is what is causing the problem."

It was a gracious observation, I thought, in a way letting the Americans off the hook. But I was unsure myself if what I had witnessed was born of fear or of hate. Vinh had come down on the side of fear, but for the millions of South Vietnamese who knew they needed American help in winning the war and preserving their freedom, the choice was never simple. I had expected Vinh to agree to my request to call the police platoon back from the operation, but it became clear that he was taking a longer view.

"Mr. Harpold, think what could have happened if you had not been there? If Redactor Thanh and his men had not been there?" Vinh said. "The police can be an example for the Americans. They can show them how to fight and respect civilians. That's why we should use the police in the villages, not soldiers. We will leave the police on the operation. When the soldiers see how the police treat the people and do their jobs, over time, the professionalism of the young Americans will improve."

Disappointed, I left Vinh's house that night feeling bad for my countrymen, sad that young Americans sent to a foreign country to help had instead found themselves trapped in situations where their morality, learned through family, church, and community, did not seem to provide solutions. An often-unseen enemy subjected them to brutal ambushes and atrocities, and their fear of the civilian population in Vietnam was not entirely unfounded. *But how do you keep fear from generalizing into the hate that underscored atrocities?* I pondered.

I attributed hate to the other side, but I had found it in my own heart as well.

15

"FRANKLY, MIKE, IT APPEARS TO ME THE CO may have been justified in opening fire on that hamlet. Your men found two armed NVA hiding in there, didn't they?" Colonel George Isley, the province senior advisor, said. "They even threw a grenade at you."

After returning from the operation with the armored cavalry troop and my talk with Chief Vinh, I had spent the rest of the evening typing up a report detailing what had happened that day: the reconnaissance by fire on the hamlet by the US troops, the slaying of the Vietnamese woman by the South Vietnamese Army interpreter, and what I troubled had been the murder of an elderly Vietnamese man by an American officer. After a few hours of sleep, I went to see Colonel Isley.

"Yes, but the hamlet was occupied by civilian non-combatants, several of whom were wounded by .50-caliber fire. He should have waited to see if we drew fire first," I responded defensively.

"He had been ambushed the afternoon before. Two of your men got killed. He was, in his judgment, protecting his men and yours," Colonel Isley rejoined.

"He violated the rules of engagement," I protested, falling back on legalism. "He had not seen the enemy and had not been fired upon."

"Mike, you've got to give the CO some slack. He's responsible for you and your men as well as his, and he's got a mission to accomplish. No commander is gonna want to have you along if you keep questioning their decisions."

"The whole idea of using the police in civilian areas is to save both Vietnamese civilian and American casualties," I countered. "And that's besides doing a more effective job of rooting out the VC that only the Vietnamese themselves can do. It's not about substituting one source of violence for another."

"Look here, Harpold," Colonel Isley flashed, "I've got to be able to call the CO of the First Cav and count on getting their help down here when we get in trouble. That's particularly important for you guys out there in the USAID compound. Something will be done about the interpreter who murdered the woman, and the lieutenant who you suspect killed an old man, that needs to be looked into. But don't expect a favorable endorsement of your criticism of that troop commander from me."

I troubled about the atrocities for many days thereafter, but another incident involving an American convoy was also very much on my mind. Forced to overnight in Tam Ky by the nocturnal closure of Route #1, the soldiers bivouacked near the bridge at the south edge of town and strung a concertina wire barricade around their trucks. In the dark, two US soldiers in search of sex walked back along the main street. Their route took them past two old men, neighbors, sitting on a log in the pleasant evening air smoking pipes. The soldiers leveled their M16s and wasted them.

By the time Vinh got word of the murders and arrived at the scene, the soldiers had returned to their trucks. Vinh went to the bivouac to talk to the convoy commander but was humiliatingly turned away at the barbwire security barricade. The officer, a major, refused to talk to him.

Vinh came for me, and I went with him back to the site of the murders. He had already collected the spent brass cartridges left on the ground, and with a flashlight, I picked up the jungle-boot tread of the two soldiers in the dirt at the edge of the pavement.

I went to see the American officer myself. I was allowed inside the wire, but the major refused to cooperate. I could not persuade him to muster his men and check for recently fired weapons, as Vinh wanted.

Stung by the rebuff, Vinh ended cooperative patrols with the US Military Police in Ly Tin village just outside the gate of the US base at Chu Lai where the convoy was headed. The joint patrols had been established to counter drug dealing and prostitution. Vinh also threatened to withhold police participation in a joint riverine patrol recently set up as part of the base defense. The province chief, Colonel Tho, backed Vinh and demanded a detachment of US Military Police be assigned to Tam Ky to police convoys traveling through town.

Atrocities were a painful topic for Americans but a very real one often discussed by the members of MACV/CORDS Advisory Team #16, civilian and military alike. Heartbreaking incidents involving the sweaty, dust-caked grunts convoying through Tam Ky and the Vietnamese children who swarmed over their trucks when they stopped too often fueled the discussions. The GIs good-naturedly bantered with the kids and gave them the candy from their C-rations. But occasionally a youth would place an M16 magazine stuffed with plastique and armed with an acid fuse on the flat top of the truck's exposed gas tank. Seven or fourteen minutes down the road, depending on the fuse, an explosion would envelope the soldiers in a fiery death.

Children sometimes died, too, shot as they ran from the trucks with purloined cases of C-rations or soda, sometimes even with the soldier's personal belongings.

At times, Doug Hostetter joined our discussions. Doug and I were polar opposites in our view of the war. He believed the United States should withdraw, leaving the people to settle the fate of their country by themselves. I saw South Vietnam as being invaded by the North in a war of conquest meant to subjugate a free people, predominately fishermen and farmers, who were ill suited to, and did not want, communism.

Yet we shared a common concern for non-combatants, and I admired the literacy and sewing projects Doug had started in the prison, practical projects that improved people's lives and reduced suffering. Doug maintained that it was resentment of the American soldiers by the family and friends of Vietnamese children that drove the kids to plant booby traps. I didn't buy that at first.

"Certainly these children can't be envious of sweaty, dust-caked grunts," I argued. "The soldiers are little better off than the kids themselves."

"True, there's not much to envy about the life of the GIs who often share treats with the children," Doug said. "But they are foreigners with overwhelming power. The children's parents and neighbors are telling the kids that the American soldiers, like the French before them, come from rich and powerful places to exploit Vietnamese resources for their own wealth, but they will soon be forced to return to their own country. Their overwhelming power, wealth, and foreignness are the reason for the resentment. The resentment eventually turns into hate. Then it's easy to recruit kids to plant booby traps."

I was reminded one noon while eating lunch at the MACV mess hall that atrocities were not solely the work of US troops. The Viet Cong fired a Soviet-made 122 mm rocket into the school across the street, destroying it. Fortunately, not fifteen minutes earlier, the children had gone home for their noon break.

My internal struggle seemed to come to a head one afternoon when I went to the province hospital in search of Dave Glennon. I had to pass through a ward filled with hurt and maimed children: infants bedded two to a cot, one on each end, their tiny, broken bodies pierced by tubes and swaddled in bandages. I had to avert my eyes and fight for composure.

"Both sides are just as culpable," Dave said. "Bullets and bombs don't watch out for the kids."

That night in my room, I wept and drank myself into a stupor. Convinced that no just God could tolerate such violence against the very innocents he had created, I told myself that if God had existed at all, he had abandoned us. Succumbing to my disillusionment, I vowed that God did not exist.

My disavowal of God left me feeling oddly liberated, as if I had just graduated from something. But in the coming days, I found I was not free of the moral and ethical obligations I had been taught in my Roman Catholic upbringing. Since God didn't exist, I no longer had him to blame for the evils I confronted. Nor was it possible to seek his help in overcoming them. That was on my shoulders alone now. I began to question my involvement in the war, but my thoughts trailed back on a conversation I had had with my family physician before I left for South Vietnam.

"We are put here to make things better," Dr. Stanley Garska had said when I had told him I was considering going to Vietnam with USAID. "The world needs good policemen, too."

Dr. Stan had been to Vietnam for extended periods on physicians exchange programs and spoke highly of the experience. He was from

Lithuania and had been sterilized by the Nazis. Socially conscious, he and his wife, also an internist, bought a home in a black neighborhood in Bakersfield. Dr. Stan's words and example made sense to me, and as days passed, they made sense to me again. I couldn't stop the war, but if I stayed involved, I could work to make things better, model morality, at least on our side.

The province chief and Chief Vinh succeeded in persuading the provost marshal at Chu Lai to assign a detail of US Military Police in Tam Ky. Although he was opposed to all US military involvement, Doug also welcomed the assignment. I encouraged Vinh to assign National Police to monitor and control the crowds that swarmed the convoys, making policing of US troops and Vietnamese kids a joint responsibility.

When sleeping space for the MPs could not be found in the MACV compound, glad to have additional help with our security, I put them up in the USAID compound. They slept on cots on our screened porches, and we shared our showers and commodes with them.

I had been too much of a patriot, too committed to the necessity of our mission in South Vietnam, and too sure of American capacity to overcome any challenge to readily acknowledge that American troops should be limited in their role. But through experience and discussions with military advisers and Doug, Dave, and Vinh, I had come to accept that there was too fine of a line between fear and hate for US troops to conduct operations in populated areas without harm, sometimes intentional, to non-combatants. Using US troops in populated villages and hamlets increased the chance of American involved atrocities.

Dealing with Vietnamese non-combatants in the rural towns and villages appropriately was the task of the Vietnamese police. Sharing a common language and culture, the National Police Field Force was far more effective than US troops in such operations. As much as I wanted it to be different, the conclusion was inevitable; to the extent possible, American troops ought not to operate in populated areas.

Believing, with some justification, that the police were ill trained, untrustworthy, and ineffective, convinced that their own troops were equipped and able to do the job, most American commanders were reluctant to ask for a unit of the National Police Field Force. But I had successes to point to, and with the goal of convincing US commanders to include the police in their tactical operations, I redoubled my efforts to ensure that both of the province's NPFF companies were trained and ready.

16

"Cô *gái Mỹ!* Round-eyed girls!" my driver exclaimed, jabbing his finger at the large, grey house sitting back from the street behind a wrought-iron gate. A lecherous grin split his youthful face. I sighed and reached behind my seat for my bag.

I had not wanted to drive down to Quang Ngai; at least the practical, sensible side of me hadn't. I had never been in the city before and knew no one. The road was dangerous, requiring the driver to pack along an M16. Worst of all, I was 90 percent certain I was about to make a fool of myself.

It was too late to turn back. Full of misgivings, I threw in with the side of me that said, yes, I really do want to talk to an American girl and share a little bit of home. I felt emotionally tired, perhaps fueled by having had to deal with incidents in and around Tam Ky that continued to trouble me, and I was concerned by a growing sense of disillusionment.

I got out of the Jeep. An aged Vietnamese man wearing green fatigues with a World War II era carbine slung over his thin shoulder appeared and swung open the gate. As if to prevent a sudden change of heart, my driver sped off.

Chief Vinh had suggested I make the trip as we stood chatting in front of National Police headquarters late one afternoon.

"Mr. Harpold," he said, "I heard there are some American girls down in Quang Ngai. Why don't you go down and visit with them?"

That Vinh would suggest I needed female companionship puzzled me. Tam Ky was very conservative, the seat of an ultra-nationalist political party, and I had avoided so much as a hint of indiscretion.

The author and Province National Police Chief Vinh..

I wondered if Vinh's concern had been triggered by a recent incident in town. The mess sergeant at the MACV compound had been sleeping with a Vietnamese woman, one of his employees in the mess hall. One night while the sergeant's Jeep was parked in front of the woman's house, someone slipped a grenade into the gas tank and blew it up.

Vinh was a devout Catholic and a family man, but he had a hint of roguishness about him, and his suggestion was enough to make me wonder about the American women. Military nurses worked at the evacuation hospitals at China Beach outside of Danang fifty miles north of Tam Ky and at the big US base at Chu Lai, about thirty miles south, but I had never considered visiting them. They were surrounded by thousands of young, mostly single, men. I was married. How would I introduce myself? What would I say? "Hi, I'm lonely?"

There was no US military base in Quang Ngai, but the women could be Red Cross workers, I thought, or work for one of several non-governmental organizations that under contract to USAID helped resettle refugees.

At USAID orientation in Washington, DC, the previous spring, I had met a group of twelve nuns, members of a nursing order, who were also bound for Vietnam. The nuns were in the charge of a French-Canadian superior, Sister Marie, an unsmiling woman who wore steel-framed glasses. One day, I struck up a conversation with one of the younger nuns, Sister Frances, and invited her for a cup of coffee in the cafeteria. My forwardness drew a rebuke from Sister Marie, and thereafter I kept a polite distance.

After two weeks, the sisters left for Hawaii to continue their training while I remained for language classes at the Foreign Service Institute.

I thought it was highly improbable the nuns could be the women Vinh was talking about and put the thought of a visit to Quang Ngai out of my mind. But the following week, Vinh brought up the subject again.

"I'll give you my Jeep and driver," Vinh said, ignoring my lack of interest. "You could drive down this weekend."

"No," I said.

I believed I had put the matter to rest, but on Friday afternoon, my secretary, Bà Mui brought it up. Mui was irrepressibly outspoken and often ribald, but now she was serious, and it was apparent she and Vinh were in cahoots.

"Mr. Harpold, I think it best you do what Chief Vinh say," she said.

"Why, Mui?" I challenged. "Why should I go down to Quang Ngai?"

"The only thing I know, my boss," she said solemnly, "is sometime a man need a woman."

I had not said yes, but on Saturday morning Vinh's driver knocked at my door. Resigned, I pulled on a tattersall shirt and my green Wrangler jeans, packed a change of clothes and my shaving kit into a duffel bag, and we were off. Two hours later, we pulled to a stop in front of the European-style house in Quang Ngai where Vinh had instructed the driver the American women lived.

Bathed in bright, late-morning sunlight, the house looked as if it had been transplanted from a residential street in Paris. The mansard roof was tiled in grey slate, broken in places. Necessitated by the war, thick sheets of opaque plastic replaced the glass in the large casement windows set in the grey façade.

Praying that my legs wouldn't crumple beneath me, I walked across the paving stones and climbed the steps to the front door. I was frantic for words to explain myself and close to panic. I knew no one inside the house, yet here I was, bag in hand, preparing to ask a group of women I had never met and who had no idea I was coming to spend the night! It was beyond anything I had ever done in my life or could conceive of doing. I felt totally foolish and imagined my humiliation if I was turned away. What would I do then? My Jeep and driver had sped off; I had no idea where. I knew no one in Quang Ngai.

Tremulously, I raised the knocker and struck it against the worn iron base. Too quickly, the heavy, wooden door swung open. A slender woman of about forty, wearing a light-colored shift, appeared in the doorway. Her short, dark hair was held in place by a white hairband. Her eyes, set behind steel-framed glasses, widened.

"Mike!" she exclaimed, her dark eyes flashing as if they were exploding star shells.

"Sister Marie!" I exclaimed.

We hugged, not a mere embrace, but a giant, crushing bear hug. Given the formality of our brief acquaintanceship in Washington, DC, the warmth of our greeting was so improbable that, only in subsequent reflection, only in the context of our utterly changed circumstances, could the spontaneity and joy of it be believed.

Sister Marie ushered me into the sparsely furnished front room. We sat in overstuffed chairs and chatted as one by one other nuns brought straight-backed chairs from the dining room and joined us. I recognized several from the group at USAID orientation. In Washington, DC, they had worn black habits; now, they wore skirts and blouses in casual, pastel colors.

Just before lunch, Sister Marie showed me up the stairs to a vacant bedroom. In the hallway, I noted recently completed repairs to the front wall and asked about it.

"One night about a month ago, a group of Viet Cong came by on the street and fired a B40 rocket at the house," Sister Marie explained. "It went right through the wall without detonating, straight down this hallway, and exploded when it hit the back wall."

"Was anyone hurt?" I asked gingerly.

"No," Sister Marie said. "It was a miracle. Sisters were asleep in the bedrooms on either side of the hall. Sister Joan and Sister Anne Marie were in the rooms at the back of the hall and were deafened for days, but we're all okay."

For our lunch, an elderly Vietnamese cook served a noodle dish and fruit cocktail from a can. We talked about their work at the province hospital, and the nuns revealed more details about their often-precarious existence. Sister Marie said that Quang Ngai was an open city, and from their sanctuaries in the heavily forested mountains to the west, Viet Cong soldiers forayed into the town at will. Often, they targeted the hospital.

The nuns said they could not remain in the hospital overnight, nor could the Vietnamese nurses they were training who feared being kidnapped and forced to work in Viet Cong hospitals deep in the jungle. The VC took all the medicine and kidnapped patients who could walk, forcing their captives to dig tunnels or carry supplies on the Ho Chi Minh Trail. During the night, patients had to be cared for by family members.

Still, Sister Marie said, they felt more fortunate than the team of Canadian doctors and nurses who operated a tuberculosis hospital in the city. Four times, the Viet Cong set explosives in the building and demolished it. Each time, the Canadians patiently rebuilt.

The nuns were concerned about my safety in Tam Ky. Surely, it was more dangerous than Quang Ngai, they said. I hesitated to tell them that our advisory team lived on the edge of the town behind a wall protected by barbed wire and claymore mines, measures not possible in the heart of the much more populous city of Quang Ngai. In contrast to the old man who guarded the nun's gate, we employed an armed, mercenary force, Chinese Nung, to protect our compound.

The nuns told me about the USAID agricultural advisor who had been murdered by the Viet Cong on the front steps of his nearby house. He was a black man, they said, a professor from a Midwestern university.

"We could hear his screams," Sister Marie said. "But we didn't dare even go to our windows. We prayed. The VC blew the house apart; not one stone was left resting on another. Then they booby-trapped the professor's body."

We passed the afternoon playing Scrabble and gin rummy and swapped anecdotes about the fate of others. In this indirect way, we talked out our personal fears, but I avoided revealing my terror of dying while I slept, of being killed by an exploding shell and never waking up.

I wondered if my presence made the sisters feel safer. I carried a small revolver in an inconspicuous holster on my belt. But, as we talked, I began to realize that their sense of security had nothing to do with me or guns; my presence was little more than the welcome visit of a big brother. The nuns could have left for home at any time; they could have caught the Air America flight to Danang that afternoon, had they wanted.

"It's God's plan that we are in Quang Ngai," Sister Joan said. "He brought us here, and we are to mend broken bodies and teach Vietnamese nurses."

"It's God's will if we live or die," Sister Marie added.

Since the despair I had experienced that night in Tam Ky after witnessing the maimed and burned children in the hospital ward, I had disavowed God. I could no longer relegate his existence with the human suffering I saw as the result of the war. In the weeks following, my resolve that God did not exist did not weaken, but I began to be affected by an essential corollary to my agnosticism: if there is no God, there can be no heaven. My newly acquired rationality forced me to shed my Roman Catholic belief in salvation and the hereafter. If I died, my soul, if I had one, would be catapulted into an empty abyss, an eternity of darkness.

I feared being killed while I slept. During the dark phase of the moon when the Viet Cong and the North Vietnamese crept close to town and dropped mortar shells on our compound, I draped my flak jacket over my body and fought sleep. I began to drink heavily.

After dinner that evening in Quang Ngai, the nuns and I walked to the province headquarters, and in a screened pavilion, we found seats on folding chairs. Others joined us: Red Cross workers, a group of Quakers, some Vietnamese families, and the Canadians. The air was warm, and a soft breeze evaporated the moisture from our skin. As darkness descended, the orange light from drifting parachute flares cast us in eerie shadows. We listened to the muffled crump of artillery in the distance, as South Vietnamese guns desultorily fired at the Viet Cong lurking in the mountains.

Into the night, interrupted only by the need to change reels, we watched raptly as projected on a collapsible screen southern ladies in bouffant gowns waltzed with dashing Confederate officers. Atlanta burned, and Rhett Butler and Scarlett O'Hara, battered by events beyond their control, fought to preserve the vestiges of their former lives. Transported deep into our personal thoughts of home, that evening we, too, dreamed of Tara.

I lay awake in bed that night reflecting on the faith that enabled the nuns to serve in this hostile place with such quiet valor. Tentatively, even grudgingly, I began to see what they saw: the simple Christian truth that through belief in God there is life after death. I felt a yearning for spiritual healing, a reconciliation with God. I found myself envying these nuns who lived and worked free from the anger that was slowly immobilizing me.

The next morning, I opened up a little to Sister Marie, revealing that my faith had strayed.

"God is always there for you, Mike," Sister Marie said when my driver appeared, and she walked me to the front gate. "Don't fight God, Mike. Let him in."

After I returned to Tam Ky, I thought a lot about the nuns and their faith. Slowly, I came to realize that through reason alone, I could never resolve the mysteries of faith and the great burning question that had driven me from God: why had we been given a free will if only to kill and main each other here on Earth?

In time, I did let God in. I no longer had to accept that my soul would be blasted into an eternal darkness, my body buried in the cold ground, a quickly decaying relic of my brief time on Earth. Lying in my bunk on moonless nights, I still covered myself with my flak vest, but I could find peace, at least until the shelling started.

I teased Vinh and Mui for sending me off to a nunnery. It drew good-natured laughter, but they were not embarrassed. They knew, and I knew, that the weekend had not been for naught.

* * *

Soon after my visit with Sister Marie and the nuns, on June 8, 1969, army nurse First Lieutenant Sharon A. Lane was on duty at the 312th Evacuation Hospital at Chu Lai, halfway between Quang Ngai and Tam Ky. The base came under attack by the Viet Cong. While attempting to move the Vietnamese patients on her ward to safety, Lieutenant Lane was killed instantly by shrapnel from a Soviet-made

122 mm rocket. She was twenty-five years old. First Lieutenant Lane was awarded the Cross of Gallantry by the Vietnamese government for her efforts to save her Vietnamese patients.

Eight thousand American women, military and civilian, served in the war zone during the Vietnam War. They were all volunteers. Sixty-eight died. Lieutenant Lane's name and those of seven other women, all nurses, are on the Vietnam Veterans Memorial. The sixty other American women who died were civilians.[1]

On February 1, 1968, during the Tet Offensive, medical missionaries Ruth Thompson, Ruth Wilting, and Carolyn Grizwald were killed during the North Vietnamese Army assault on the leprosarium in Ban Me Thuot. Betty Ann Olsen was captured but died on the Ho Chi Minh Trail. Six years earlier, Eleanor Ardel Vietti was taken prisoner at the leprosarium by the NVA. Her fate is unknown, and she is listed as a POW/MIA.[2]

In 1972, Evelyn Anderson and Beatrice Kosin were taken prisoner when the NVA assaulted Krengkok, Laos. The missionaries were kept bound to the corner post of a house for five days. Not wanting to impact incipient peace talks in Paris, Pentagon officials declined to mount a rescue mission. The NVA set the house afire, burning the women alive.[3]

In May 1975, during the evacuation of Saigon, thirty-seven American women died in the crash of a C5a transport plane. Evacuees themselves, the women had volunteered to care for the over two hundred Vietnamese orphans on the flight who also perished.[4]

1. "1. Lt. Sharon Anne Lane," accessed April 9, 2012, angelfire.com/ne2/slane/.
2. Michael Benge, "The Last Witness," The Alliance, accessed April 9, 2012, http://www.cmalliance.org/alife/the-last-witness/.
3. "Beatrice Kosin," Task Force Omega Inc., April 9, 2012, taskforceomegainc.org/ka01.html.
4. "1. Lt. Sharon Anne Lane."

17

On a sunny Saturday afternoon in April, Hoang's fiancée, Cô Hai, set off on his Honda motorbike to visit her family in Tien Phuoc. The Viet Cong controlled the road, but once every two weeks, US tanks and armored personnel carriers escorted a convoy of trucks and buses the fifteen miles to the isolated district town. Pushing the capability of the armored vehicles to protect them, Vietnamese riding motorbikes often surged a short distance ahead and then waited for the slower convoy to catch up.

Cô Hai was very slender, weighing less than one hundred pounds. Well ahead of the protection of the tanks, a Viet Cong sniper laced her side to side with an AK-47. When the convoy arrived at the scene, the Americans medevacked her to the hospital at the US base at Chu Lai.

Mui came running to my house with the news. I drove immediately to Chu Lai and found Hoang already at the hospital. Cô Hai was out of surgery and would live, but Hoang was distressed.

"Mr. Harpold," Hoang exclaimed, "they take out her spleen and throw it away. They take out her liver and throw it away."

A nurse tried to explain that Hai could live a normal life without her spleen and part of her liver, but in Hoang's Confucian/Buddhist belief system, the removal of her body parts was a desecration. Unwhole, she could not enter heaven.

Hoang and Cô Hai's misfortune didn't end there. Weeks later, a special unit of the South Vietnamese Military Police, the Quân Cảnh, swept Tam Ky, searching for draft evaders, and arrested Hoang. Reacting to charges in the stateside press that multitudes of young

Vietnamese men strolled the boulevards of Saigon while young American men, drafted in large numbers into the war, bore the brunt of fighting in the jungles, Ambassador Bunker urged President Thieu to crack down. In response, Thieu dispatched the Quân Cảnh to cities and provinces to search out and arrest draft evaders. In their net, they rounded up not only deserters but also every young man of military service age not already in the armed forces. Both Hoang and Chief Vinh were detained. Vinh was spared when the province chief, Colonel Tho, bestowed on him the military rank of "aspirante," cadet.

Despite his USAID employment in the war effort and his usefulness to me, Hoang was shipped off to a South Vietnamese Army post. It happened on a weekend, and I did not learn of it until Monday. By then he was gone, and I had no opportunity to see him. I had not realized that Hoang was a draft evader, thinking that as a USAID employee he must have had an exemption. Learning that he didn't, I accepted his conscription as legitimate.

Police Special Branch Chief Nghia and Hoang.

I missed Hoang as both an employee and friend, but his departure did not cripple my efforts. Having attended Michigan State, Chief

Vinh spoke excellent English. Others on his staff, as well as one of my National Police Field Force commanders, spoke English to varying degrees. When my command of Vietnamese was insufficient, at least in my office and at province headquarters, I could use Bà Mui.

But the Quân Cảnh raid had other repercussions.

Learning of the sweep in advance, Jerry Dobbs, the deputy province senior advisor, hid his "personal assistant," Mr. Long, in his house. The morning after the Quân Cảnh left Tam Ky and Long resumed his duties, he abandoned the USAID van at the airfield and then hopped aboard the Air America aircraft for its return to Danang, stranding arriving passengers as well as leaving the arriving mail. There, he turned himself in to the astonished Vietnamese policeman posted in the lobby of the USAID headquarters.

Enraged at the loss of Mr. Long, rebuffed by the province chief when Dobbs asked him to intercede, Dobbs directed me to instruct my counterpart, Chief Vinh, to contact his superior, the Region I National Police chief in Danang, and get Long released. I refused. I had no direct authority over the police chief, anyway. Colonel Isley then asked me to intercede. Again, I refused.

Hoang had been arrested because Ambassador Bunker insisted that President Thieu crack down on draft evasion. Having accepted Hoang's fate and the government of South Vietnam's primacy in the matter, I did not want to send a mixed message to Vinh. As a plebe at West Point, I had been required to memorize Worth's Battalion Orders, "An officer on duty knows no one—to be partial is to dishonor both himself and the object of his ill-advised favor." It had turned out to be sound guidance for my service as a border patrol officer and as a public safety advisor as well. I expected the same level of integrity of Vinh and the National Police.

I suspected Long had good reason to want to leave his employment with USAID, and it was not probable he would voluntarily return to Tam Ky. Colonel Dobbs was an ill-tempered man and a bad drunk. Using USAID funds, he had remodeled a house for himself a couple hundred yards from the USAID compound, turning it into a walled chateau. He stayed out of my Public Safety activities, but I had to deal with him in matters relating to the administration of the USAID compound. One night in a drunken rage, for no apparent reason other than he hated the Nungs, Dobbs rode his motorbike to the USAID compound and beat up Hau, our Nung guard captain.

I was away with the NPFF, but learning of it after I returned, I confronted Dobbs and demanded that he stay away from the USAID compound. I complained to Colonel Isley, who told me there was nothing he could do, that Dobbs had powerful friends in the USAID hierarchy in Saigon. From that point until the day he asked me to intervene to free Mr. Long, Dobbs and I stayed out of each other's way, but he made it clear that he would not forget my insubordination.

Several weeks after Hoang left in the custody of the Quân Cảnh, I had a visit from him, now wearing the dark-green fatigues of the South Vietnamese Army. He had been assigned to a nearby unit and was expecting to be utilized as an interpreter by the South Vietnamese Army. He invited me to roast a dog that evening with his brother. I was glad to see him and wanted to spend the time with him, but having experienced eating dog meat the night of my first operation with NPFF in Danang, I did not want to do it again. I politely declined.

18

LATE AFTERNOON HAZE HUNG OVER the distant Annamites, and the setting sun, grown large as it began its drop beyond the curvature of the Earth, turned an angry red. Across the abandoned railway tracks from the USAID compound, sparse savannah, melancholic and empty, stretched to the distant line of foothills. Beyond sight, US fire support bases that protected Tam Ky were already under siege. There would be no moon that night. *A perfect night for an attack on the town*, I thought as I turned into the driveway.

Inside the walls, birds nesting in the small trees chirped lyrical evening songs, but they did not dispel the anxiety that had fallen over us. For several days, the MACV intelligence officer had reported a North Vietnamese buildup, the prelude to an attack. Carl Harris, a Unitarian minister who worked in the refugee program, took his bedding and moved to the greater security of the MACV compound. Two other advisors, whose wives lived in USAID safe-haven housing in Bangkok and Taipei, had already departed on the afternoon Air America flight for a well-timed visitation.

I worried that the headspace on our four WWII-vintage, .30-caliber machine guns was set right. After disassembling the gun for cleaning, the barrel had to be screwed into the chamber until it was fully seated and then rotated back two clicks. If not, the gun would be prevented from firing. The odd, nagging thought had bugged me all afternoon, but the possibility couldn't be ignored. When I left police headquarters, I stopped by the Tactical Operations Center for the latest briefing and alerted the duty officer that we would be test-firing our guns that evening.

Jim Daw was outside when I arrived at the compound and went with me to explain to Captain Hau that I wanted the machine guns test-fired. The Nung chief fired a burst in the air from each gun in turn, startling the other Americans who popped from their rooms, flak jackets, helmets, and weapons in hand. Sheepishly, I apologized for not alerting them in advance, but I took the moment to relay the most recent intel.

"Yesterday afternoon, the VC shot down a large, twin-rotor Chinook helicopter attempting to land at Landing Zone Professional about five miles west of here," I explained. The US basecamp was on a pair of distant hilltops, low, grey silhouettes on the horizon. "Soon after, a North Vietnamese unit attacked the LZ. The battle has continued for twenty-four hours now, and LZ Professional is in danger of being overrun.

"The North Vietnamese force includes the Third Regiment of the Second Main Force NVA Division and a host of lesser Viet Cong units, including a sapper battalion. The size of the force is large enough to indicate they plan a direct assault on Tam Ky. The attack could come tonight."

Reassured that our guns would work when needed, I concluded we were in as good a shape as we were going to be. Preparing for another night in the bunkers, the pragmatists among us went to bed early. Others, eschewing sleep, nevertheless paced their drinking.

Just before dark, Deputy Chief of Police Thieu came for me, and we joined a police patrol on the western edge of Tam Ky. Open fields and rice paddies surrounded the city, and although roads into town were barricaded at dusk, no walls or barbed wire protected the town from an assault. Guarding against infiltrators depended largely on the willingness of the occupants of the thatch houses in the neighborhoods at the edges of town to report them. We walked from house to house along winding footpaths, and the police compared the names of the occupants of each dwelling with the family census book.

Mr. Thieu and I broke off from the patrol to join another that was checking establishments, somewhat akin to homeless shelters, that provided sleeping space for itinerants and truck drivers traveling on

Route #1. Finally, at full dark, we checked the police-manned strongpoints in the city, rooftops of buildings overlooking intersections, and sandbag emplacements at strategic points along the thoroughfares. Each site was manned and the police alert. All seemed to be in readiness, and at about midnight, I asked Mr. Thieu to take me back to the USAID compound.

I lay fully clothed on my bunk and had barely dropped off to sleep when the first mortar shell exploded in the compound. It did no damage but brought us racing to the bunkers. The night quickly got noisy. The battery of eight-inch guns behind us roared to life. Small-arms fire crackled from the direction of the airport. We watched the green tracers of Communist guns rake the hilltop outpost above province headquarters about a mile northwest of us. The concrete and sandbag fortification at the top was manned by a South Vietnamese Regional Forces company with a MACV advisor. Angry red tracers streamed back down the slope at the attackers.

In the moonless sky above, a Spooky gunship droned, executing an elongated loop extending from the besieged hilltop outpost to the savannah and low hills to our front. We had as yet to receive any direct fire, but the pattern flown by the gunship indicated the controllers, using radar and infrared devices, believed there were enemy troops to our front. As the Spooky circled, its Gatling guns spewed a stream of red-orange tracers to the ground. The roar of the guns arriving in our ears seconds later sounded like a prolonged fart.

"It's like a giant is up there in the clouds taking a piss," I remarked to Jim Daw who along with Chief Hau crouched beside me in the bunker.

"Yeah, and he's got a big bladder," Jim quipped.

A mortar shell buried itself in the sandy earth of the driveway but failed to explode.

I climbed down to check in with the men crouching in the other wall bunkers. After making my rounds, I climbed back up to the front wall bunker, but before I could get off the ladder, a mortar shell exploded in the soil at the base of the bunker. The blast threw up a plume of shrapnel and sand, stinging my neck, ear, and the side of my face and nearly knocking me from my perch. I felt a sharp pain, like the sting of a hornet, above my right eye. That afternoon, I went to the province hospital, and a Vietnamese surgeon cut a tiny sliver of metal from my upper eyelid.

About three in the morning, muffled by the din of the guns, we heard the creak of tracked vehicles approaching. Just visible in the dim illumination at the outer limits of our security lighting, a ghostly procession of armored assault vehicles from the First/First Cavalry Squadron crept along the road in front of us. The tracked vehicles turned off the road and took up positions facing west along the railroad tracks.

After a long night, as dawn approached, the fighting quieted, but other than what we could see and hear, we had no way of knowing what was going on. We relied on a hand-held police radio for emergency contact with the MACV compound, but it was on a civilian police frequency and was considered too insecure to be used for relaying news.

I needed to go to the tactical operations center to check in and get a briefing, but first we had to clear the unexploded mortar shell buried in the driveway. The shell's vanned tail protruded from the sand, and one of the MPs crawled to it and dropped a noose over it. After it was pulled from the soft earth, an MP detonated it harmlessly with a round from his rifle.

The streets of Tam Ky were deserted as I drove to the TOC, but I did not see a lot of damage. I was relieved to find that the prison, which sat exposed behind province headquarters, was secure. In an attack the preceding spring, the Viet Cong had succeeded in breaching the wall and freeing over three hundred prisoners.

I pushed through a blackout curtain into the claustrophobic, heavily sandbagged room that housed the TOC. I was surprised to find a slightly built civilian with a receding hairline and clear plastic–rimmed glasses standing among the Vietnamese and US military officers there. He wore dark dress pants and a white shirt but no tie. I was reminded of a banker or accountant who had just arrived at his suburban home and was about to mow the yard before dinner.

"Mike, this is Ambassador Colby, the head of the Pacification Program, your boss," Colonel Isley said. "Mr. Harpold is the Public Safety advisor for Quang Tin Province," he explained to the ambassador.

"How do you do?" the ambassador said with a warm smile, extending his hand. I was astonished to learn Ambassador Colby had slipped into town unannounced the previous evening and spent the night in the TOC with Colonel Isley and Colonel Tho.[1] He didn't volunteer it, and I didn't think it appropriate to ask why he had come to Tam Ky at such a dire moment. I turned instead to Colonel Isley for a briefing on our situation.

"We lost every outpost to the town in the first half-hour of the NVA assault last night," Colonel Isley said. "We had to fire illumination rounds over them and get an O1 Bird Dog up to fly low enough to try to figure out what was happening on the ground."

"We could see the battle for the hilltop behind province headquarters," I said. "But we couldn't tell what was going on."

"We lost that one, too," Isley said. "We had to send a pair of armored personnel carriers up to rescue the survivors and Captain Allen, their advisor. They had to fight their way through phalanxes of North Vietnamese troops to reach the summit and then fight their way back down again. At the outpost west of the airport, the advisor, a captain, was the sole survivor."

"We saw napalm being dropped out there," I said.

"You did. The advisor survived crouched in an eighteen-inch-wide slit trench. We thought he was lost, but he was able to walk down off the hill just a little bit ago."

Colonel Isley asked if I would let Ambassador Colby use my room to shower and shave. I was happy to, of course, and we left for the USAID compound in my Jeep.

---

1. Ambassador Colby, along with Ambassador Ellsworth Bunker and General Creighton Abrams, managed US efforts in the Vietnam War in 1969 and after. Abrams was commanding general of Military Assistance Command Vietnam, while Colby directed Civil Operations and Revolutionary Development Support (CORDS), the joint US Vietnamese pacification program, which included the Phoenix program. Before arriving in Vietnam, Ambassador Colby had been deputy director of the CIA. At the end of the war, President Ford appointed Colby CIA director.
Ambassador Colby began his legendary intelligence career in the Office of Strategic Services during WWII. In 1944, he parachuted into Nazi-occupied France to organize and train the French Maquis in sabotage. After the Germans were driven out of France, Colby parachuted into Norway to organize the sabotage of railways to prevent Nazi divisions from returning to Germany to participate in the final defense of the homeland.

19

IN THE COUPLE OF HOURS WE SPENT TOGETHER, I found Ambassador Colby quiet but inquisitive. He asked me multiple questions about the police program, and soon I found myself sharing my experiences with US units on joint cordon and search operations.

"Ambassador, we can save many civilian and American lives and spare US troops from charges of atrocities if we simply use the National Police Field Forces in villages and hamlets," I said. "They speak the language, they're part of the culture, and they, rather than US forces, are best able to identify and dig out the Viet Cong infrastructure."

"One of the things I like about my job," the ambassador said after hearing me out, "is that everyone who works for me believes that with a little more emphasis on his program we can win the war. The agriculture guys say that with the new types of American rice we're importing, South Vietnam can feed most of Asia. The rural development guys say we can defeat the Viet Cong by stringing electric lights in every village. These are all great ideas, and I support them, as I do yours.

"I think you will be pleased by a couple of things coming down the road shortly that will involve the National Police," he added cryptically.

Thanks to the timely arrival of the First of the First Cavalry during the night, we still held the airstrip, and an Air America C-45 was able to land to retrieve Ambassador Colby. While we waited, huge four-engine C-130s began to arrive, making little more than touch-and-go landings, disgorging troops of the First Brigade of the 101st Airborne Division from their rear cargo ramp before taking off again.

Just hours before the paratroopers landed, they had been engaging the enemy west of Dong Ha, one hundred miles north. That afternoon, they began pushing back the North Vietnamese Army west of Tam Ky. Over the next three days, over 1,200 men from the 101st and their equipment would land in Tam Ky.[1] With their arrival, and the arrival the first night of the US First/First Cavalry Squadron from Hawk Hill, the already hard-pressed 196th Light Infantry Brigade was reinforced, and the brunt of the fighting and the momentum shifted to the American units.

Heavy fighting raged for weeks in a narrow valley between Tam Ky and Tien Phuoc that became known as Death Valley. The bulk of the enemy force was forced to grudgingly fall back towards sanctuaries in the mountains to the west. Despite the loss of the outposts, with the help of airstrikes, artillery, and Spooky gunships, the North Vietnamese assault had been checked at the outskirts of Tam Ky.

There were many funerals in the days that followed for the Regional and Popular Forces soldiers who had borne the brunt of the fighting that first night. The Ruff-Puffs, as their American advisors called them, were recruited locally to protect their hometowns and villages.

In the weeks following the attack, elements of the NVA and the VC continued to threaten Tam Ky, launching probing and harassing attacks almost nightly. A VC unit hit a strong point in the southeast part of town manned by the National Police Field Force but was repelled with many casualties.

Still, life went on as usual, a fact that heartened me every time I pondered the uncertain future of the South Vietnamese people. Children carrying briefcase-like plastic book bags lined the streets of Tam Ky on their way to school the morning following the attack, spending that day and the days to come sitting in rows at bench desks, reciting their lessons in unison for a teacher standing in the front of the open-air room.

In the daytime, the American advisors went about our usual tasks, but the VC continued to fire mortar rounds into the USAID compound, forcing us to spend much of the night in the bunkers. One night while we were at our posts on the wall, a Viet Cong 82 mm mortar round hit one of the prefabs. The shell pierced the thin aluminum

[1] The battle for Tam Ky, in military parlance, Operation Lamar Plain, would last for three months. The First Brigade of the 101st suffered 521 casualties.

roof and detonated on the concrete floor just outside the bathroom. The explosion ripped through the thin veneer wall destroying the toilet and blasting thousands of pieces of jagged porcelain shard through the two adjoining bedrooms.

A Presbyterian minister from Philadelphia who worked in the refugee program lived in one of the units, and all his personal possessions were destroyed. Every handkerchief and every sock was holed by the porcelain shrapnel. His suitcase shredded and useless, the reverend, a dignified, middle-aged man, gathered the remnants of his belongings in a white bed sheet. That afternoon, carrying his bundle over his shoulder like a hobo, he boarded the Air America flight to Danang. The pressure of living under siege was taking a toll.

The Viet Cong sporadically attacked the assault vehicles and tanks arrayed along the abandoned rail line in front of the compound with rockets and grenades, hoping to inflict casualties among the cavalrymen who bedded down on the bare ground between their vehicles. One night, they shelled the tracked vehicles with white phosphorous, Willy Peter, in grunt jargon. Its hotly burning chemical crystals burned through flesh and bone and could not be extinguished by water. Foxhole lore said to douse the wound in beer. Able to identify the enemy attackers on their night-vision scopes, the assault vehicles returned fire.

We hit the bunkers, but a few minutes later Chief Hau grabbed my arm and urgently jabbed his finger towards the driveway. Chris Soderberg, a Foreign Service officer who worked in the refugee program, had let himself out the front gate and was strolling towards the tanks that were furiously firing back at the attackers with machine guns and cannon. He was bareheaded, wearing a white, short-sleeved shirt and khaki pants, and nonchalantly carrying a scotch and soda in his hand. I jumped down from the bunker and raced out the gate after him.

"Let go of me," he yelled as I grabbed his arm. "I'm a diplomat! I can go wherever I want! You can't stop me!" White phosphorus was exploding in massive fireworks-like plumes among the armored vehicles not thirty yards in front of us.

I grabbed Chris in a headlock and dragged him back into the compound. He continued to protest each step of the way. I left him at our aid station in the center bunker with Dave Glennon and returned to my post.

A few minutes later, the Nung chief nudged me again. Chris was back at the gate and about to exit the compound a second time. This time, Dave and I tied him by his wrists and ankles.

Chris had graduated from an Ivy League university prior to being accepted in the US Foreign Service and had led a sheltered suburban life. Gene Chiperelli, who headed the refugee program, taught him how to drive on the airport runway. I taught him how to shoot, but the only weapon I had available to give him was a vintage Thompson sub-machine gun.

Despite having the sympathy and help of every one of us, Chris was having trouble finding his place among us. One night as we had secured after an alert, Chris had jumped down off his bunker, accidently firing a burst into the ground beside the foot of one of the MPs. The soldier had yelled at him angrily, drawing an emotional response from Chris who had felt himself aggrieved. Looking back on it, I thought his outburst that night might have been the prelude to his behavior the night the tanks were attacked with white phosphorous.

In the morning, I went to see Colonel Isley. Chris had tried, but it had been too difficult a transition from a sheltered, university campus existence to life on the barricades in Tam Ky. He was a danger to himself as well as to us. He left on the Air America flight that afternoon, still protesting my abrogation of his rights as a diplomat.

The platoon of tanks and assault vehicles of the First/First Cavalry remained out front for several weeks, and we shared our hot showers and flush toilets with the troopers. But this time they had brought a surprise for us: a case of vodka.

"We don't mind rolling down to Tam Ky in the middle of the night to save your butts," a trooper said. "But when all you have to offer us to drink is crème de menthe, that's somethin' else!"

Thanks to the generosity of the tankers, now we could mix the crème de menthe with vodka and drink it over ice. In honor of the donors and their life-saving tanks, we dubbed the concoction a "German."

20

THE MOON, A BRIGHT, SILVER DISK, REIGNED HIGH in the cobalt sky, and the half-dozen or so Vietnamese police officials and I sipping cognac or drinking beer in the quiet evening air on the darkened patio behind Chief Vinh's house found it impossible to avert our gaze. Although we could not possibly see the *Apollo 11* spaceship and the lunar lander Eagle, Neil Armstrong and Buzz Aldrin had begun their descent to the sun-bathed lunar surface. In the magic of the historic event, we shed our nationalities. WE were about to land on the moon.

Radio Hanoi said the moon rocket had crashed. The Viet Cong claimed the *Apollo* astronauts had never left the Earth, that the moon mission was faked, but no one believed the Communist propaganda. Our attention, and that of the people of Tam Ky, was fixed on the drama that on that night would write a new chapter in the history of mankind.

"Maybe the astronauts will find Chang'e, the lady who lives on the moon," Mr. Ban quipped. In Chinese legend, Chang'e swallows the pill of immortality given to her husband, the archer Houyi, by the Jade Empress and becomes light-headed, floating off to the moon.

"When Chang'e reached the moon, she coughed up the pill, and ever since, the hare has been trying to pound it back into shape," Mr. Dinh said, leaning over to me and pointing to the shadows on the lunar surface. "You can see the rabbit's ears for yourself."

"I heard the lady was the emperor's fiancée," I said, recalling a tale related by the cultural secretary at the Vietnamese embassy to our language class at the Foreign Service Institute. "They had a quarrel, and she went off to live on the moon. The emperor's subjects lit lanterns and formed a long procession so he could go to the moon and be with her."

"That woman's name was Cuoi," Mr. Thieu corrected. "She urinated on the roots of a magic tree and then climbed onto a limb. The tree grew until it reached the moon. At the Autumn Têt, the people form a procession of lights to show her the way home."

That night, the *Apollo* and the Eagle proved the credence of millenniums-old folk tales.

In South Vietnam that summer, other big changes were underway. On June 8, 1969, at a meeting with President Thieu at Midway Island, President Nixon announced the Vietnamization of the war and the eventual withdrawal of all US combat troops. The first drawdown of twenty-five thousand troops would be accomplished in July and August. Henceforth, the United States would engage in limited offensive operations, and emphasis would be placed on the Pacification Program, winning the war through expanding Government of South Vietnam control over the countryside and eliminating the infrastructure that allowed the Viet Cong to exist and conduct operations.

In Quang Tin Province, government officials were at first surprised and then shocked. The very term, Vietnamization, implied that the Vietnamese people had lost control over their own destiny and the Americans had usurped direction of the war. The province chief, Colonel Tho, met behind closed doors with province officials and political leaders for three days of intense soul-searching. No Americans were included. The morning following the meetings, Chief Vinh came to my office.

"Mr. Harpold, we know that you Americans are leaving," Vinh said. "We need all the help you can give us before you go."

That night over beer at the MACV club, we found similarity in the reactions of each of our counterparts: shock that the Americans were leaving and a renewed commitment to ensure that South Vietnam succeeded on its own.

I welcomed the news, convinced that the commitment by both countries to the joint pacification effort promised success. From the outset, I believed that the South Vietnamese needed to be made so self-sufficient that American advisors could be kicked out of the country and nationalism grown so strong that we would be stoned as we made our way to the airport.

By late July, enduring heavy casualties, the First Brigade of the 101st Airborne Division and the 196th Light Infantry Brigade had driven the North Vietnamese Army far back into the Annamite Range along the Laotian border, and Tam Ky was no longer directly threatened. The road to Tien Phuoc was opened. Security had improved that summer, paddy fields reclaimed.

Colonel Tho planned a sweep north of Tam Ky through an area of rice paddies and hamlets used as a staging area for attacks on the town and asked the National Police Field Forces to accompany the First/First Cavalry in the operation. Chief Vinh assigned both companies. Probing the ground, the roots of trees, and clumps of foliage in advance of the tanks and armored assault vehicles with sharp-pointed canes fashioned from rebar, the police discovered many Viet Cong spider holes, capturing or killing the occupants. The tactic preempted the VC from popping up between two armored vehicles from their hidden positions in an attempt to provoke fratricidal fire, a hazard in sweeps conducted by armored units not supported by infantry. A new arrow was added to my quiver of arguments for utilizing the police.

In the wake of the Vietnamization announcement, US commanders sought NPFF units for operations in populated areas. The Marines launched a six-day sweep operation on the coast in much the same area as had the First/First earlier in the year, this time sweeping into the province from the north. Chief Vinh and the Special Branch Police accompanied a company of NPFF, setting up an interrogation and intelligence center to screen suspected VC and Viet Cong infrastructure, villagers who set booby traps, acted as lookouts, or supported the Viet Cong shadow government and were captured in the sweep. He set up a briefing tent for visiting brass, complete with bulletin boards displaying photos and flow charts and a white board with up-to-the minute statistics. The Marine Corp brass loved it.

New emphasis was placed on the Phoenix Program, the joint US/Vietnamese effort to neutralize the Viet Cong by killing, capturing, or converting its soldiers and destroying the infrastructure in the villages and hamlets that supported them. Heretofore, the responsibility for the program lay entirely with the Central Intelligence Agency, which not only gathered the intelligence but also reacted to it with its mercenary force, Provincial Reconnaissance Units (PRU).

With the deployment of National Police Field Force platoons to district towns earlier in the year, and the newly announced program to deploy the National Police to the village level, the NPFF was in a position to react to intelligence developed by the Police Special Branch. Ambassador Colby had promised I would be pleased to see "a couple of things coming down the road for the National Police." Indeed, I was. Vinh and his staff worked assiduously to implement the new programs.

Security had improved enough in most areas to permit the deployment of the white-shirted National Police to the villages, but mountains of difficulties remained. The villages had responded well to programs initiated by the national government to improve local security. With arms supplied by Saigon—critics had said President Thieu would never arm the populace, but he did—the South Vietnamese government recruited and sustained Popular Forces platoons and Village Popular Self Defense Forces, which became the model for the police deployment. Encouraging also, the National Identity Card program had succeeded. Despite threats from the Viet Cong, thousands of villagers in Quang Tin Province and elsewhere showed up to fill out the required information, be fingerprinted, and have their photos taken.

But as I had often found in Tam Ky, two steps forward often triggered a step back. One afternoon in July, about a month into the village deployment program, I chanced to drive by Mr. Nghia's house. I was surprised to see scrap metal being unloaded into Mr. Nghia's yard from the police five-ton truck and stopped. Mr. Nghia was the Police Special Branch chief and a good friend of Chief Vinh. Unexpectedly, Vinh stepped into the street.

"Mr. Harpold," Vinh said unconvincingly, "we've found roofing for our village police stations." At first I was puzzled but then dubious. Building police stations was in the plans, but USAID wasn't going to roof them with scrap metal.

Several days later, I discovered the truth. I remembered an American contractor searching for Vinh at police headquarters one afternoon. He had not come by my office, and I wondered what his business had been. Belatedly, I asked Mui.

"Mr. Harpold, the man give Chief Vinh scrap metal, and he sold it for twenty thousand dollar American money," Mui said.

"Why?" I asked at the jaw-dropping news.

"The police in Ly Tin District arrest forty truck drivers at Chu Lai as draft evaders, and Chief Vinh let them go when he get the scrap metal," Mui said, quickly starting on another task.

"I need the money to buy a promotion," Vinh said when I confronted him. "It's the way things are done in Vietnam."

I was aware of the practice, common in Asian and developing nations, but had yet to be actually confronted with it. With Vinh, I'd thought it impossible. Vinh had been penniless when he had come to Tam Ky; he and his family had slept on mats on a concrete floor. Further disadvantaging him, he was a Catholic in a predominantly Buddhist hierarchy. Charlie Sloan, an avuncular executive in the USAID Public Safety program in Saigon, who had mentored me when I had arrived in the country, selected Vinh, then a promising young police officer in Saigon, to attend Michigan State University under USAID sponsorship. That Vinh had stooped to corruption broke my heart, and I could never mention it to Charlie.

USAID had educated Vinh to be a future leader in a western-style meritocracy that did not yet exist in Vietnam. I could understand that and understand the twilight existence of his generation of young, government leaders as they sought to break from the corrupted Mandarin system of the past and establish a civil service that was accountable to the people and bound by the rule of law. I could not equate Vinh with Captain Ha, who filled the coffers of high-ranking army officers with the proceeds of prostitution. Yet I was filled by idealism, too. Taking from the people you were there to protect, even if they were American companies, was wrong, and I could not find it within myself to forgive Vinh.

Although we continued to work together to build a police force and defeat a common enemy, in my remaining months in Tam Ky our relationship remained strained.

Vinh and I had reached an East/West divide that neither of us was able to cross. He and his country were going to have to work such things out themselves, I concluded.

21

Change swept through US Army Vietnam in the spring and summer of 1969 impacting MACV/CORDS Advisory Team #16, too, often in unanticipated ways. Some of the new measures would create tensions between the military and civilian sides of the overall advisory effort that would prove difficult to overcome. The ground was shifting beneath my feet as well. In Tam Ky, the new marching orders for the army translated into the assertion of hierarchical control over the development programs that USAID brought to the team.

Colonel Isley was rotated out, replaced as province senior advisor (PSA) by Colonel Farley. I had gotten along well with Colonel Isley, whom I could sit down with shoulder to shoulder in the MACV mess hall or over a beer in the club. But Colonel Farley was imbued with the new regimen, and to see him, I had to first go through a captain, also newly arrived. Farley expressed little interest in the Public Safety program. The young captain, astonished to find a civilian working for him in the war zone, knew nothing about the police and had to be told what the abbreviation USAID stood for.

I viewed CORDS, Civil Operations and Revolutionary Development Support, as an umbrella for autonomous organizations in USAID and MACV, working in discrete programs. Although I rarely saw or heard from him, my immediate superior was the chief of Region 1, USAID Public Safety Division in Danang. Recognizing that we were integrated into a structure paralleling the provincial government in Quang Tin Province, I carefully coordinated my activities with all the other USAID and MACV advisors in the province. But the new PSA had a different view.

Under the new regimen, control over the Air America Helio Courier I chartered weekly from my USAID program funds for my transportation and to transport supplies and replacements to the police garrison in isolated Tien Phuoc was to be given to the PSA, his deputy Colonel Dobbs, and the new captain, the self-proclaimed "Head Shed." They, not I, would decide the mission and by whom the four-seater aircraft would be used. Although I had always been open to sharing the resource with other programs, and often did, I refused to cede control of it.

An Army Civil Affairs unit arrived in Tam Ky, and I was asked to share my small office—the space was provided by the National Police, not USAID—with a sergeant and a private. The private, a draftee, enthusiastically helped out in every way he could, mostly running errands or accompanying me in the field. I could have used a good infantry NCO to help train the NPFF, but the sergeant was not that. Most of the tasks I asked of him, he passed on to the private. He mostly sat and looked at me or read a paperback. Mui ignored him.

Returning to my office unexpectedly late one morning, I found the sergeant sitting behind my desk, shirt off. He jumped up, but did not have time to remove the memo he was working on from the carriage of my typewriter. It was addressed to his superior, the commanding officer of the civil affairs company. Unbelievably, it referenced the sensitivity of his mission to report on my activities and promised he would continue to keep him informed.

I ordered the sergeant out of my office and delivered his memo to his CO myself. I told the red-faced captain that I welcomed his civil affairs organization's assistance but not his meddling. I never saw the sergeant again, but I let the private stay.

By 1969, the war had stretched on longer than had the direct involvement of US troops in WWII or Korea, and the military brass worried about the impact on morale. For the first time in history, narrated by an increasingly critical press, the US public viewed a war on the TVs in their living rooms. In Vietnam, the GI newspaper, *Stars and Stripes*, carried stories of anti-draft demonstrations and riots at home. Draft resistance was increasing, home-front support for the war weakening.

But those weren't the only problems we heard about. Newspapers from home featured front-page photos of race riots in major cities and articles about the growing drug culture. The one-year rotation of troops, many conscripted, meant that young soldiers were arriving in Vietnam having experienced those things, and the brass worried that new recruits would bring drug and race problems to Vietnam, too. I had seen little or no evidence of either in the army and marine units I worked with, let alone in MACV. Still, commanders felt they had to initiate measures to strengthen the glue that held units together and sustained their performance. That glue was discipline, which military commanders, alarmed by incidents such as the massacre of civilians at My Lai and the fragging of officers, felt to be in danger of slipping.

The army began enforcing what were popularly known as "chicken regs." Grooming and dress standards were enforced; officer courtesy was required. At the MACV mess in Tam Ky, hastily installed railings divided seating into three sections: enlisted men, NCOs, and junior officers. Field-grade officers ate behind a partition in the rear of the room.

Puzzled by the new protocol, there was no designated section for civilians; we plopped down our trays in one or the other of the officer sections. But when we joined the majors and lieutenant colonels dining behind their new partition, we drew a cold shoulder. We shrugged and ate our meals at the enlisted men's tables.

Similarly, the small MACV bar was now the officer's club. A storeroom was cleaned out to make way for an NCO club. Feeling that we were being eased out, civilians avoided the officer's club unless invited. We set up a bar in the front room of my house, stocking it from PX runs to the US bases at Chu Lai or China Beach.

Apart from a weekly staff meeting, the MACV mess and club had been the natural gathering places to plan and coordinate as well as to get acquainted with one another. MACV province and the district advisors in Quang Tin Province were a constantly changing cast. Typically, army officers were rotated every six months while civilian USAID advisors could, and often did, serve in the province for two years or longer. Intentional or not, segregated dining tables and clubs made the day-to-day working relationships between the military and civilian members of the joint advisory effort more difficult.

Colonel Isley had served as a foil between the advisors and his nominal deputy, retired Colonel Jerry Dobbs, but under the new centralization of power, Dobbs was suddenly involved in our activities. Bounced from job to job in USAID and finally exiled as a problem employee to Tam Ky, he had taken on no advisory role. Instead, he contented himself with our administration, controlling all the USAID funds coming into the province and attending to the details of our housing and locally hired Vietnamese employees. I was thankful that Dobbs housed the dozen third-country nationals, Filipinos and Koreans, employed by USAID to build and run the telecom aspects of the Public Safety program, in his compound. It saved me a huge amount of administrative bother. But I was often concerned for their safety.

Dobbs had built octangular-walled turrets with red-tile roofs above the whitewashed walls on either side of his front gate, giving the place the look of a French Foreign Legion outpost in the Sahara. It was only a matter of time before the Viet Cong used them for target practice, and late one evening they fired a B40 rocket into one of the turrets, killing the guard inside it, an old Vietnamese man. Not one to bow to a threat, Dobbs had the turret rebuilt.

On the positive side, in July, a former Special Forces sergeant, hired by Colonel Grieves in Saigon, was assigned to me to help with the National Police Field Force. With the increase in joint operations with US units and the increased role of the NPFF as the reaction force in the new Phoenix Program, designed by the CIA to identify and kill, capture, or convert the participants in the Viet Cong infrastructure, his assignment was a welcome addition.

In August, a newly hired Public Safety advisor, Orval Delfous, arrived from Danang as my assistant. We were roughly the same age and hit it off well. It was the week also that the MACV club got a new allocation of hard liquor, this time a pallet of rum.

The brother of a friend and neighbor in Bakersfield had just arrived on Hawk Hill for service with the First/First and in a letter home complained about not being able to get rum. I bought two bottles from the MACV club's stock, and on Saturday afternoon, Orval and I drove up Route #1 to the firebase.

We hadn't quite gotten there when we saw a green-and-white police Jeep stuck in loose sand off the shoulder of the road and stopped.

A policeman was out on the road waving his revolver in the air trying to get a passing vehicle to stop. He was staggering drunk. Some US Navy Seabees in a three-quarter-ton truck pulled up behind us, and for a moment, we ignored the drunk policeman while we helped the Seabees hook up to his Jeep.

A civilian bus passed up the policeman but stopped at his angry shouts. A Vietnamese soldier jumped out of the back and grabbed the M16 I had left in my Jeep, leveling it at the policeman. Orval and the Seabees dove for cover, but I climbed back up the bank, grabbed the policeman in a headlock, and wrenched his revolver from his hand. Dragging the policeman with me, I approached the startled soldier and grabbed back my M16. I told the soldier and the astonished bus driver to get on their way. I was very relieved that no one had been hurt, particularly with my gun, which I felt I had left carelessly exposed. Orval and I were happy to finally get to Hawk Hill and locate the young GI.

But I suspected that Orval's arrival was handwriting on the wall, that my tenure in Tam Ky was about to end. I had been in Tam Ky for eleven months and felt I had been largely successful. On the Vietnamese side, with newfound vigor, confidence, and resources, the police and prison programs had blossomed. But because of the growing bureaucratization and the sense that I had lost the support of the MACV/CORDS hierarchy in Tam Ky, Colonel Dobbs, and now Colonel Farley, told me it was probably time for me to move on.

Two weeks later, glum-faced, Mui handed me a teletype from Wally Burmeister, newly arrived Public Safety boss in Danang. She had read the message. I was directed to proceed to Quang Ngai that afternoon to fill in for the Public Safety advisor there who was on home leave. On his return, I was to report directly to Danang for reassignment.

It didn't take long to pack up my things, and that afternoon, as I was preparing to leave for the airport, Mui and her husband came by my house to see me off. Vinh came also.

"Mr. Harpold, you will always be my advisor," Vinh said, apologetically. But I had not forgiven him for his shakedown of American contractors at Chu Lai. We shook hands and embraced each other. Vinh again assured me that in spirit, I would always be his advisor. But I was not sure if he had failed me, or I had failed him.

Little was said when I eventually arrived in Danang, but a performance evaluation from Advisory Team #16, dated some weeks earlier, awaited me. In typically military phraseology, it read: "Mr. Harpold considers command guidance simply unnecessary interference and reacts accordingly."

Fair enough, I thought.

22

After reaching Quang Ngai and finding the Public Safety advisor's house, I had time only to check in at province headquarters and visit my friends, the nuns, when I was stricken by a bout of dysentery. The advisor whom I was to fill in for, Steve Donnelly, had already departed on home leave, but his maid continued to come to the house daily. She proved to be an incompetent cook, however.

What little appetite I had for food vanished when she brought me what appeared to be a wet, reddish-orange crêpe burnt around the edges. I asked her what it was. After a moment, she reappeared with an empty Campbell's tomato soup can. She apparently had not added water as the directions required, frying the contents of the can in a pan.

I dosed myself with tetracycline, the all-purpose antibiotic given me at my briefing with Colonel Grieves at National Police Field Force headquarters in Saigon almost a year before. Sister Marie and a Quaker lady dropped in often with soup and food, but I didn't improve. On the tenth day, I had an unexpected visit from another US advisor apparently sent from Public Safety headquarters in Danang since no one up there had heard from me.

My visitor gave me two little green-and-brown balls about the size of BB shot. It was raw opium, he explained, the base of the prescription anti-diarrhea medicine, paregoric. He promised me that ingesting it would not make me high, and it didn't. My stomach cramps disappeared. That evening, I was up and around and enjoyed a meal and a visit with the Canadian doctors and nurses who worked at the TB hospital.

When Donnelly returned, I flew up to Danang and reported to my new boss, Wally Burmeister, chief of Region 1 PSD. Wally was a retired executive from the New York State Troopers, new to Vietnam, and still getting his legs. There was no room for me on the organization chart, he said. All the province jobs were filled, as well as the advisory slots at Region I National Police Directorate. I was an extra hand. In a country at war, I had not thought that possible.

I was sent first to Hue and next to Quang Tri, the province bordering the Demilitarized Zone, to fill in for advisors on home leave. Since each of the assignments was for only three weeks, it was barely possible to learn the names of the Vietnamese officials I was to work with, let alone build a relationship that would get anything done. Between such assignments, I did what I could to be useful in Danang.

I worked for a while with the Marine Police, patrolling the Danang River, boarding and searching sampans and junks for Viet Cong and contraband. That ended abruptly one Saturday afternoon. In preparation for an inspection, the police had cleaned the engine with gasoline that morning. Later, preparing to cook a meal, they lit a hibachi on the rear deck igniting the fumes that had accumulated in the bilge, and their lone patrol boat exploded and burned to the waterline.

Learning that the police needed furniture for a new training room at their headquarters, I got USAID funds to buy lumber and build desks and chairs. Working with US Navy, Marine, and Army supply officers, I arranged for the National Police in province and district towns to draw stores of sandbags and barbed wire from surplus supplies at US bases.

Burmeister had little curiosity about local government affairs in Danang, and soon I was replacing him on a joint committee to coordinate aid to civic projects in the city. The committee included representatives from the US military, American voluntary aid agencies, and representatives of the many other nations who sent assistance to the Vietnamese in one form or another.

The French had called the port city Tourane and built a row of handsome, white, three-story administrative buildings with red-tile roofs fronting a broad avenue paralleling the immaculately manicured waterfront. Reminiscent of Paris, the avenue had been lined with chestnut trees, but strangely the magnificent trees were dying.

Agent Orange was suspected, but no one knew how the defoliant was reaching the trees or what to do about it. The exhaust of the hundreds of Honda motorbikes that clogged the avenue from early morning to late evening was suspected, but it was pointed out that vehicle exhaust had not destroyed the trees that lined the Champs Élysées in Paris. The problem was put before our committee.

We learned that the Vietnamese commonly bought gas for their motorbikes on the black market. Despite frequent patrolling, the venders were able to tap into the petroleum pipeline that had been hastily built aboveground to transfer gasoline and jet fuel from tankers in the harbor to the Danang airbase. Black marketeers drilled holes in the pipe and siphoned off gasoline into fifty-five-gallon drums. When we learned that most of the drums were scavenged from an air force dump and had previously contained Agent Orange, the mystery was solved. The toxic motorbike exhaust was indeed defoliating the trees.

We prevailed on the air force to crush and bury the empty Agent Orange barrels, but it was too late for the trees. The magnificent chestnut trees so reminiscent of Paris to the French residents of Danang had to be cut down.

An assignment to evaluate the diversion of USAID Food for Peace commodities to the black market also fell to me. The burlap bags of bulgur wheat and corn-soya meal displaying the USAID logo, clasped hands over a red, white, and blue shield, were found for sale in every open-air market in Vietnam. The bulk food commodities were meant not to be sold but to be distributed free to starving people.

Despite the war, Vietnam continued to be a rice exporter, and except to feed refugee families, there was little need for the imported food. The USAID imported corn oil could be used for cooking, but bulgur wheat and corn-soya meal were unknown in the Vietnamese diet. Consequently, the agencies that distributed Public Law 480 commodities, the Red Cross, Catholic Charities, and Church World Service to name just three, searched for Vietnamese to distribute it to.[1] Every policeman and civil servant in Danang received a monthly allocation, as did all who simply came to the organization's warehouse

1. Public Law 480, enacted in 1954, created the Office of Food for Peace and expanded international aid in part with surplus American products.

and asked. The bags of wheat and meal were swapped in the market place for rice.

But the food was not going to waste. Rice farmers took the bulk commodities home and fed them to their hogs. Pork production soared. I estimated the diversion at close to a million metric tons, almost all the bulk Food for Peace commodities arriving through the port of Danang in 1969. USAID responded by sending an additional million metric tons to "make good the loss."

I missed Tam Ky and, despite the insecurity, the satisfaction of working in that isolated province with my Vietnamese counterparts and the Americans with whom I had shared common goals and dangers. One morning I received a visit from a policeman from Tam Ky, Mr. An. I questioned him about Bà Mui, Hoang, and Vinh, but he soon revealed a far more urgent and personal reason for his visit.

"Mr. Harpold, please help me," Mr. An pleaded. "My nine-year-old daughter is very sick, and we fear she is going to die."

I did not recognize the Vietnamese word Mr. An used to describe his daughter's illness, but from his description, it sounded as if the girl had lockjaw. He had brought her from Tam Ky to the Vietnamese hospital in Danang, but she had gotten progressively worse. When told that her death was inevitable, he had taken her back to his family who had come to Danang also.

Mr. An asked me to take his daughter to the US hospital at China Beach. She would have received care there, I knew, but instead I thought of the German hospital ship, the *Helgoland*, as a more likely provider of the treatment she would need if such were possible.

The Helgoland had three operating rooms and 130 beds. Ten German doctors and thirty nurses cared for sick, hurt, maimed, and burned Vietnamese civilians. It docked in Danang during daylight hours but at night moved offshore out of the range of the rockets the Viet Cong and North Vietnamese fired randomly into the city. I had met the captain at the civic action committee meetings and had visited aboard, leaving well stocked each time with Heinekens.

I went with Mr. An in my Jeep and waited at the end of a winding lane while he went to get his daughter. He returned carrying the pajama-clad girl on his back. Her spine was bent into a rigid arch, her limbs stiff, her jaws locked in a hideous grimace. I helped him arrange her stiffened body across his knees in the back seat.

My heart in my throat, balancing her body across my arms like a board, I carried the child up the gangway of the *Helgoland*. Unable to move, unable to even whimper or cry, the terror in her eyes was the only sign that life existed in her small, frozen body.

That night, I wrote home and asked my family and my friends to pray. In the weeks following, I visited the *Helgoland* often, bringing small gifts and stuffed toys.

Thanks to massive doses of horse serum administered by the doctors, she lived, and after about six weeks on the *Helgoland*, Mr. An was able to take her home. She sometimes stumbled and seemed silly, Mr. An reported, but his family was happy to have her alive.

The doctors and nurses on the German hospital ship Helgoland cared for sick and wounded Vietnamese civilians, moving offshore at night for safety and returning to its berth each morning in the city of Danang.

23

I PRESSED MY FACE TO THE WINDOW of the Northwest Orient DC-8, anxious, even in the predawn black, to get my first glimpse of home. As the aircraft began a long, low approach towards SeaTac airport in Seattle, Washington, I could make out strip malls, parking lots, and the neon lighting of an all-night café. Occasionally, a car's headlights illuminated the snow-covered highway below. The aircraft straightened, paralleling an arterial street. We were low enough now that I could see snowflakes falling under the streetlights.

Flaps down, engines powered for a landing, we cruised just a few hundred feet above the ground, over darkened houses their roofs outlined in red, green, blue, and white Christmas lights. Strands of multi-colored bulbs draped the snow-laden limbs of conifers. Outdoor crèches and lighted snowmen stood vigil on front lawns. Wreaths graced front doors. Curtains pulled back revealed lighted Christmas trees, and in at least one home a lighted menorah, in the windows of darkened living rooms. Occasionally, a lighted kitchen indicated life was astir, a mother or father preparing breakfast before heading off to work or getting kids ready for school.

Why are their Christmas lights still on, I pondered? At our house, we turned the tree lights off before going to bed. Our neighbor's outdoor displays were generally dark by eleven, certainly not left on all night.

It occurred to me at first as an errant fancy that I quickly dismissed. But then I remembered nearby Ft. Lewis and the thousands of servicemen and women who passed through SeaTac on their way to and from Vietnam. The warm Christmas greeting sent up to us by the residents of the work-a-day neighborhood below was not a dream. *They've left their lights on for us!*

I was in an instant exhilarated, and then I cried. Those of us who served in Vietnam that Christmas of 1969 had read reports of antiwar protests and student riots at home in the armed forces newspaper, the *Stars and Stripes*, and in letters from home. America was turning against the war, we knew. Soldiers traveling in uniform were met with cold stares. The polite ignored them. Stories circulated overseas of GIs being jeered and spat on. Although I was not traveling in uniform, I wondered what to expect when I arrived home.

But in the homes beneath our landing path, south of SeaTac, families had left their lights on for us! That simple, heartfelt welcome home meant the world to me that Christmas, and I would never forget it.

My arrival home in Bakersfield, California, that afternoon seemed especially joyous. After three weeks' leave, I would return to Vietnam for several more months, but the bulk of my long absence was past, and our family was starting look to the future.

Miki was ten, a blonde, long-legged, skinny-Minnie wearing a red mini-skirt and white knee socks. Shelly was eight, Katie was seven, and neither had her permanent front teeth yet. I searched for a measure of the impact of my absence on them, but thinking about it was hard.

Before I left, I had tried to explain about Vietnam and why I felt I should go, leaving them alone in Bakersfield for two years, an almost incomprehensible length of time at their age. I had put Miki on one knee and Shelly and Katie on the other.

"Daddy, what are you going to be when you grow up?" then nine-year-old Miki asked when I had finished. Shelly and Katie had puzzled looks.

Dominica, who had been listening from behind my chair, turned away, hiding a smile. Taken down a notch, I smiled, too. We had planned that talk for days, but in the end it served only as a reminder that our daughters were very young and that my absence could not be taken for granted, a simple turn in their lives that they would age past.

Katie was six and a first-grader that fall when I first arrived in Tam Ky. One morning, she took a picture of some American soldiers fighting in Vietnam to school for show and tell. She told her classmates and Mrs. Noble, her teacher, that her daddy was in Vietnam. She started to cry. When Mrs. Noble cuddled her, the teacher later related to my wife, Katie said she wasn't scared for her daddy but the lights in the classroom hurt her eyes. Dominica had waited until I was home before telling me, but it was a searing reminder that they struggled to cope with their daddy's absence.

From left to right: daughters Miki, Katie, and Shelly with the author on the steps of a beach house in Morro Bay, California, while the author was on home visitation.

We had a little extra money that Christmas. My salary with USAID was about ten thousand dollars a year, around 10 percent higher than my border patrol pay, and with all our girls in school, Dominica found a job in a photography shop. I had stopped overnight in Hong Kong before boarding a flight the next morning for Tokyo and then on to Seattle. After checking into the Peninsula Hotel, I hopped on the crowded Star Line ferry to the Kowloon side and the China Fleet Club, the British Royal Navy Exchange. There, I browsed through seven floors of jewelry, china, stereos, clothing, and toys.

I bought elaborate Japanese dolls for Miki and Shelly, geishas in colorful, silk kimonos, and glass and lacquered-wood cases to display them. For Katie, I bought a baby doll in a silk kimono, one that she could cuddle. On a whim, I bought a cuckoo clock to hang in the girls' bedroom, but the cuckoo proved to be an annoyance not even they could tolerate, and they hung a blanket over it. I bought a strand of Mikimoto pearls for Dominica.

In those pre-free trade years, prices at the exchange were about 40 percent of those in the States, and we decided to buy a component stereo system: a tuner-amplifier, turntable, reel-to-reel tape player, and four speakers. I didn't stop there, adding a set of Noritake china and stainless steel dinnerware to my purchases.

The gifts were packed in sisal-filled wooden crates and delivered to a freight dock at street level where porters waited in a line. I motioned to the first three men, paying each five Hong Kong dollars, about sixty cents, to carry the boxes next door to the post office. Conveniently, a Chinese man loitering in the lobby sold me a black marker pen, and I scrawled our address on the wooden slats. The horde of booty arrived in time for Christmas.

On Christmas Eve, Dominica gathered the excited girls in the kitchen while I helped Santa Claus arrange the gifts under the tree in the living room. Then I joined them for a family tradition, the reading of the Christmas story from the New Testament. There were groans when I started from Matthew.

"Daddy, not the begats again!" the girls protested.

They settled down when I skipped to Luke and started again with the visitation of the Archangel Gabriel. Our family reconnected that Christmas, and Dominica and I attended a succession of holiday parties with old friends.

Fulfilling a long-held ambition, I decided to learn to fly a sailplane while I was home. Each day while Dominica was at work, the girls and I drove up to a glider school in the Tehachapi Mountains, forty miles from Bakersfield. The girls sat longingly in the car while I soared high above, first with an instructor and then solo, and they laughed and waved excitedly each time I bounced along the ground in a typically novice, bumpy landing.

I tried to make the trips worthwhile for them with plenty of ice cream and hot dogs. I promised to take them up once I got my license, but when I saw there would be neither enough time nor money for me to reach that stage, I paid for them to go up with an instructor for a ride of their own.

Too soon, it was time to return to Vietnam.

24

When I got back to Danang, I picked up a new assignment. In 1969, the National Police began deploying to the villages, and US and Vietnamese officials and planners at all levels were anxious to see how the program was working. The Region I National Police Directorate organized an inspection team to go from village to village and take a look. Mr. Toan, the well-respected and long-serving chief of the National Police in Quang Nam Province, was selected to head the team. Two young redactors, Nguyen and Thanh, were assigned to assist him. I was asked to accompany the team as their US advisor and to evaluate and report on the deployment for the US side.

Historically, the national government did not reach into the villages. An ancient Vietnamese maxim held, "The king shall not pass the village gate." Villages were self-governing with a popularly elected council and president, a tradition that was respected by the South Vietnamese government. But South Vietnam's emergence as a modern nation, governed by the rule of law and accountable to the people, required that national law be enforced in villages, too.

The new, joint US/South Vietnamese Pacification Program called for giving the people responsibility for their own security by arming and organizing villagers into local Popular Self Defense Forces. The initiative by the central government was a success. The next step was to recruit policemen locally, train them, and organize them into National Police units at the village level,

Mr. Toan, a stocky man with close-cropped, grey hair, looked powerful and fit in his brown-and-tan camouflage National Police

Field Force uniform. He spoke good English, the two redactors less, but my Vietnamese was good enough to make sense of most of what I heard in briefings. My reputation from Tam Ky preceded me, and when asked by host police organizations what accommodations the team's American advisor would require, Toan answered, "None, he eats and sleeps just like us."

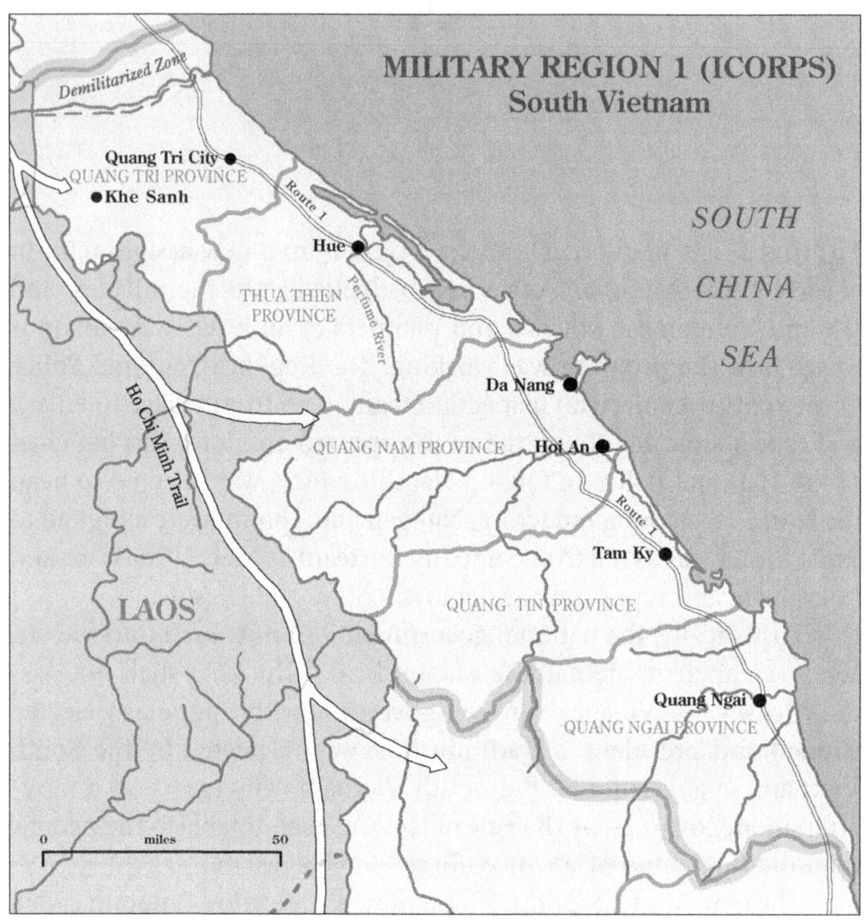

Military Region 1 (ICORPS)

We started off in Quang Nam Province, close to Danang, traveling mostly by Jeep but also by motorbikes and sampan when necessary. We spent a half-day in each location, sometimes overnighting in the village we visited in the afternoon. We ate and slept in the homes of the local police.

On the first night, the housewife spread a single, cotton sheet on the tabletop for me, while the family, Toan, Nguyen, and Thanh included, curled up together on a mat on the floor. I spent the night listening to their snoring while I shivered under the thin cover and tried to find a comfortable position on the hard tabletop to relieve the throbbing in each of my joints. Thereafter, I carried along a poncho liner, but I remained envious of the tangle of warm bodies huddled together on the sleeping mats.

The new National Police posts were generally located in already existing village buildings; some were constructed of concrete, but many were wattle and thatch. Typically, the local police chief conducted the briefing with the aid of a map and a chalkboard. Mr. Toan and I were seated side by side, and he made sure I did not miss the mention of any equipment or facility needs. While we listened and asked questions, we were served a can or bottle of Coca-Cola. At the end of the briefing, the police officers, dressed in white shirts, grey trousers and caps, as in the province and district towns, formed up in front of the station for a photo.

Next, we visited the village chief, invariably a young, energetic civilian as opposed to the military officers who were frequently placed in charge of districts and provinces by the national government in Saigon. Aided by the fact that most of the officers had been recruited locally and the noticeable improvement in local security in the spring of 1970, most were supportive of the National Police presence.

At the last, reaching the top of the local hierarchy, we were introduced to the village council, old men wearing white, black, or grey ao dais and turbans. They were the Mandarins; long nails curved from their little fingers to establish they no longer did physical labor. Grinning from mouths stained black and red by betel nut juice, some with a few strands of hair stringing from a mole on a cheek, each in turn bowed and clasped my extended hand in both of theirs.

The author's host family for a night in Thua Thien Province. The wife spread a sheet for him on their table.

Lunch was served in the home of a local policeman. I was surprised at how the food and manner of preparation varied from place to place. A slice of pork in Quang Ngai was trimmed to include just a thin layer of fat. In Quang Tri, five provinces north, it included not only the fat but also the rind and bristles.

Particularly in his old stomping grounds of Quang Nam Province, the tour seemed like old home month for Mr. Toan, and he reveled in his near-celebrity status. When we reached Thua Thien Province and visited the magnificent palaces built by the ancient emperors along the Perfume River west of Hue, he relished his role as our tour guide. We spent whole afternoons exploring each of the imperial estates while he lectured Nguyen, Thanh, and me on the history and significance of the long-ago ruler.

In Quang Tri Province, we visited an outpost at the Demilitarized Zone and, through binoculars peered at the red flag with a single yellow star of North Vietnamese atop a tall pole on the opposite side of the demarcation line. We spent a night in a schoolhouse in the village of Khe Sanh where the Marines had been besieged just two years before. As I fell off to sleep, I listened to the sound of artillery fire from the direction of the DMZ and the Laotian border, virtually the only sounds of war we heard on the entire inspection trip. Peace had settled over the countryside that spring, but South Vietnam was still pressed on its borders.

My time in Vietnam was fast drawing to a close, and there was a lot to be hopeful about that spring. Between January and late May, we visited over one hundred villages and did not encounter a single, significant enemy incident. Everywhere, farmers wading behind water buffalos tilled rice paddies.

In rural Vietnam in the spring of 1970, life for rice farmers was returning to normal.

We were winning the Pacification War; over 90 percent of the population that spring lived in secure towns and villages. The deployment of the police to the villages was part of that success. In the countryside, the Phoenix Program—the National Police Field Force providing much of the reaction forces—had all but eliminated the Viet Cong as a threat. President Thieu had initiated a long-awaited land reform. The country would for the first time vote for a president that fall in a free election.

One evening while staying in a village along the coast in Thua Thien Province, we heard shots from the direction of Route 1, about a half-mile away. Soon, a policeman came and got us. When we reached the site, we found a US Army Jeep that had rolled over, one of its wheels coming to rest squarely on the chest of a dead American officer. A sergeant who had been driving the Jeep, his leg broken, lay on the road clutching his M16.

The sergeant told us they were from the 101st Airborne Division at Phu Bai. The officer, a young lieutenant, was supposed to catch the Freedom Bird leaving from Danang Air Base that night, but they had gotten a late start. They ran into a barbed wire barricade, stretched across the road by the police at dusk, and the Jeep rolled. A medevac chopper picked up the sergeant and the body of the officer.

I thought about my trip home at Christmas, about the lights left on for us by the people beneath our flight path when we landed in Seattle, a sight the young lieutenant would never see. It was sad, as sad as I had found the death of the young Vietnamese boy rushing heedlessly to get a piece of candy who was crushed under the wheels of a dump truck on my first day in Tam Ky.

It was close to dark when we walked back to the village. My companions were affected by the young lieutenant's death, too.

"We are very sad at the death of the young officer," Toan said, "particularly because he was so close to seeing his home again. Who could not be saddened by that? All Vietnamese are saddened by the deaths of young Americans who come so far to help us," he added. "We know that many in the US are angry about the death of your young men, but we are sorry for their deaths too."

One morning, a couple of days before I left Danang, my boss, Wally Burmeister, and I were invited to the National Police Headquarters. In front of a National Police Field Force Honor Guard, the director presented me with the National Police Medal of Honor, Second Class. It was a high honor; the first class medal was awarded only posthumously.

"What'd you do to get that?" Wally demanded as soon as we were clear of the building. Wally was a deskman and too happy to have me out from underfoot to care much about what I had been doing.

"I dunno, Wally," I shrugged. "But obviously the Vietnamese think I've done something."

25

In late May 1970, on a warm Friday evening in Washington, DC, I walked up Twentieth Street past the George Washington University campus. After a series of long flights, first across the Pacific on Pan American from Saigon to San Francisco and then on to Dulles Airport, I had arrived too late the previous night to celebrate my first night home. After a day spent checking in at the Office of Public Safety headquarters at the State Department, I returned to the Francis Scott Key Hotel, changed into the more stylish of the two new suits I had acquired during an overnight stopover in Hong Kong, and headed out for a French restaurant on Pennsylvania Avenue.

Posters advertised a Chuck Berry and Bo Diddley concert on the campus that evening. Although I knew a lot had changed on the home front in the two years I had been gone, I was unsure of the extent. But I thought it remarkable that college students liked the two musicians whose popularity, I had thought, had waned even before the war. The new rock 'n' roll was imitated at USO shows overseas by Asian Elvis Presleys, Connie Francises, or Monkees lookalikes. Some of the blatant drug messaging left me uneasy, but I liked much of what I heard.

At the restaurant, I ordered a Chateaubriand and flirted with a pretty, blond, French-speaking waitress who helped me with the menu.

It was dark when I left the restaurant and strolled back up Pennsylvania Avenue on the way back to my hotel. As I got close to the university, the avenue was crowded with anxious, young students. The air seemed charged, the youths on the verge of panic. I smelled tear gas, CS, the same as we used in Vietnam to clear Viet Cong tunnels.

Panicky students pushed past me and tried to get into a brightly lit ice cream shop. The manager barred the door and locked it. The teargas burned my eyes, and I joined the students banging on the door. The manager relented and let us into the air-conditioned interior.

The students talked apocalyptically of Kent State, where two weeks before, the National Guard had killed four students and wounded nine others on the campus. They feared a similar event was about to happen on the George Washington University campus.

When the tear gas abated, I left the ice cream parlor and crossed Pennsylvania Avenue onto Twentieth Street. Amid the smell of tear gas and acrid black smoke, students milled about in the hellish illumination of burning vehicles and piles of trash. I watched as students rocked cars onto their roofs and torched them. They were older models, compact Fords and Chevys, the kind students or teaching assistants might drive and could ill afford to lose. In front of a row house, four or five girls with long, straight hair tugged at a section of wrought iron fence, wrenching if free, and adding it to a trash barricade the rioters were erecting. They were liberating the campus, the girls said.

I continued down Twentieth Street past a residence hall. Without warning, tear gas canisters came in from a very high trajectory; I never saw the policemen who fired them. I'm uncertain what happened next, but I found myself on my back on a grassy bank next to the sidewalk. Students wearing white medic coats were bent over me with squeeze bottles, washing my eyes with a saline solution. They helped me to my feet. Protesting that I was all right, I stumbled along the sidewalk to the next block and the Francis Scott Key.

My room was on a front corner on the second floor, and I had left the windows open. It reeked of CS. I didn't turn on the light. Bathed in the ambient light of the burning trash piles and cars, I sat cross-legged on the floor in the middle of the room and listened to the shouts, the shattering of glass, and the police bullhorns warning the students to disperse. Finally, I heard the rhythmic slap of batons against gloved palms and the measured stomp of a platoon of riot police as they pushed up the street.

I sat on the floor for a long time, until well after the shouts of the police and rioting students quieted away. I didn't try to sort anything out. It was as if I was watching a house burn down and it was mine. I felt detached, like a spectator, but in my heart, I was sick. I felt sad and afraid for my country.

Saturday morning dawned bright and clear. A breeze had cleared away the gas and the acrid smoke of the night before. Across the street in front of a church, men in tuxedoes and dark suits and women in expensive dresses gathered for a wedding. It was as if the hellish scene of the previous night had been just a bad dream. But it hadn't.

At the corner, pedestrians in casual clothes, as if on their way to a picnic, crossed through the intersection in front of a formation of leather-jacketed riot police carrying riot batons. Some of the throng carried signs saying: "U.S. Out of Cambodia" and "Stop the Genocide in Vietnam."

I was reluctant to be counted as part of an antiwar demonstration, but I was more anxious to know what was happening in my country. I went down to the street and followed the crowd towards McPherson Square and the White House.

The White House was protected by a double row of city buses parked bumper-to-bumper, so close that a human body could not squeeze between them. I followed the crowd down a side street past the Old Executive Office Building. A stage had been set up across the street on the Ellipse. The people in the audience were predominantly white and middle-class. Most appeared to be professional people: government workers, teachers, lawyers, and college students.

Speakers representing seemingly improbable coalitions harangued the crowd. Doctors of divinity with high-sounding names, learned professors from Ivy League universities, and dignitaries whose names meant little to me railed against the Cambodian incursion and American involvement in Vietnam. People listened quietly and clapped politely, as if from some sense of obligation. They appeared somewhat bored, I thought, as if they had heard these speeches too many times before. Nevertheless, each new speaker strived to build up enthusiasm.

Before I left for Vietnam, male college students, sticking it in the eye of parents who had served in WWII, were already burning their draft cards, but while I was away, the antiwar movement appeared to have spread to just about every segment of society. As I stood in the crowd listening, I began to understand why, and it was disquieting. The speakers were parroting the propaganda line I had seen and heard from Communist and North Vietnamese sources: the peace-loving Vietnamese people have chosen their government and only the imperialist, reactionary, United States was standing in the way of their legitimate aspirations.

The speakers knew nothing about Vietnam and the life the Vietnamese wanted for themselves: the people wanted to rid the country of their former colonial masters, yes, but they did not want to swap for the yoke of Communist dictatorship. Vietnamese peasant farmers and fishermen knew well the fate of their counterparts in China and the Soviet Union when new Communist masters collectivized crops and catches; the people starved. A million Vietnamese, most of them Catholic, had fled to the South at the time of the partitioning in 1954.

Ho Chi Minh had imposed collectivization in the North, and if his attempts to invade the South were successful, he would do it again. The South Vietnamese did not want to be Communist, but journalists who had made little attempt to understand the Vietnamese people were creating their own narrative of the war.

In Southeast Asia at that moment, US forces had crossed into Cambodia and were at last clearing out the North Vietnamese from their sanctuaries. I cheered the news; the United States was finally taking off the gloves and waging a real war against the Communist aggressors. But the speakers tried to incite the crowd otherwise, conjuring up images of saffron-robed monks heedlessly slain while at prayer in tiered pagodas and railing at what they called a barbarian invasion of a peaceful country.

A bearded young man wearing a dark-green army fatigue shirt—bright-yellow chevrons indicated his service had been early in the war, if at all—described American troops firing on defenseless Vietnamese women and children.

"How horrible," a woman standing next to me said. "But I guess we have to hear things like this to get our troops out of there."

"It happens," I said cautiously. "Sometimes it's inevitable when troops are trying to defend themselves."

"Well we shouldn't be there at all. It's a civil war," she said knowingly.

"It's a defensive war," I corrected. "South Vietnam is being invaded across its borders."

The woman's husband gave me a nervous look and touched her arm.

"I lived and worked with the Vietnamese for the past two years, and they don't want to be ruled by the Communists," I said, but the couple had started to move on, and people within earshot were looking away.

I had heard enough and drifted over to a sidewalk café on Pennsylvania Avenue next to the National Theatre. While at the Foreign Service Institute, on warm summer evenings, my roommate and I had often walked there from our apartment across the Potomac in Arlington and watched the crowds leaving the theatre. Attempting to reprise those pleasant moments, I ordered a shrimp cocktail and a beer.

26

ON MONDAY MORNING, I BEGAN TO SERIOUSLY address my future. The war was over for me now. I had done my duty, served my country and my generation. Now it was time to get on with my life and become simply a husband, father, and good citizen.

The USAID Office of Public Safety had offered safe-haven housing for my family in either Bangkok or Taipei if I signed on for a second tour in Vietnam. But I had promised my family I would be gone for no more than two years, and I declined. Since I was not going to return anyway, I volunteered for a reduction-in-force termination—like the army, Public Safety was scaling back—and as part of my checkout in Washington, OPS gave me two weeks to either find a new job or exercise my re-employment rights with the border patrol. I decided first to explore other options.

I visited other federal law enforcement agencies but received no encouragement. I went to the new Federal Law Enforcement Assistance Administration, reasoning that they were the domestic equivalent of USAID Public Safety and could make use of my experience. The executive who interviewed me seemed ready to help but never returned my calls.

My time in DC about to end, I went to the central office of the US Immigration and Naturalization Service on D Street, next to Capitol Hill, and found my way to the Border Patrol Division. After explaining that I had just returned from Vietnam and wanted to reinstate in my old job, I was ushered in to see the chief, Bob Stewart, and his deputy, Robin Clack.

"Welcome back, Harpold," Clack said heartily. "You've got a good reputation with us, and we want you to know that you've got re-employment rights."

I was encouraged that they seemed to remember me, the more so because they were aware of their legal obligation to give me my job back. The border patrol in the 1960s had fewer than 1,400 men, and the year before I left for Vietnam, I had earned a Sustained Superior Performance award. Fewer than a dozen such recognitions were awarded each year, and recipients were marked for advancement.

"Where would you like to go?" Clack asked.

"Well, my family stayed at my old station in Bakersfield while I was gone," I pointed out. "I'd like to just go back to work there."

"Bakersfield?" Clack interjected. "We don't have any vacancies in Bakersfield. We filled your position long ago. How about Tacna, Arizona. Eamon Mann is down there. You know Eamon."

Yes, I knew Eamon, and I had no desire to work for him in a four-man office in a remote border outpost. But it had not occurred to me that I might not be reinstated in Bakersfield. The station had grown exponentially in the two years I was gone, and I had heard from my old supervisor that officers transferred in an out frequently. I temporized while mulling over the turn of events.

"I heard the border patrol got an upgrade while I was gone," I said. "Will that apply to me?" Again, the answer was unwelcome news.

"That's right, Harpold," Stewart said. "After you've been back for a year, you'll qualify for a GS-9 just like everyone else now."

I knew that was wrong. Like returning GIs, I was entitled to upgrades or changes in benefits I would have received had I not left for service in Vietnam.

"What about AUO?" I asked.[1] "I was getting 15 percent AUO when I left."

"Well you know how that works, Harpold," Clack said patronizingly. "After you work six pay periods, you can qualify again."

My shock was tempered only by my disbelief. The number one and number two men in the border patrol were telling me I could have my job back but only if I started over again at an entry-level

1. Administratively uncontrollable overtime. Border patrol inspectors were paid an additional 15 percent of salary to compensate for all the overtime their duties necessitated.

grade and for less pay. I knew what they were telling me was wrong, but it was clear I was in for a fight to get back in the patrol.

It was lore in the border patrol that if you left you could never return. But I never could have believed that after two years' service in Vietnam, service the US government officially encouraged by granting me re-employment rights, that I would encounter a problem getting my job back.

"What about my family?" I asked. "They stayed in Bakersfield the whole time. Are you going to pay their way to Tacna?" It was at least a four-hundred-mile journey from Bakersfield, and we had furniture and household goods to be moved.

"Why don't you ask the State Department?" Stewart said. "Maybe they'll pay to move your family down there."

There was fat chance of that, I knew. I stood up to leave. I didn't offer my hand, and neither did they.

"Harpold," Stewart said, looking at me coldly, "good, loyal Americans stayed right here in the United States."[†]

I was too stunned to answer. As I walked up Pennsylvania Avenue past the White House to the Francis Scott Key, I could not believe what I had just heard. Stewart and Clack were notoriously conservative East Texans, the top two men in a federal law enforcement organization, and hardly to be equated with the antiwar crowd demonstrating at the White House. Yet their attitude towards my service seemed no different.

I pondered what to tell Dominica and the girls. Tacna, Arizona, was a dusty little town of fewer than five hundred people fifty miles east of Yuma. Miki was eleven and in another year would start junior high. Michelle would enter the fourth grade that fall and Katie the third. What kind of schools would the tiny, remote desert town offer? I didn't mention it when I called home that night.

Tacna was a line-watch station like Calexico, California, where I had started in the patrol nearly eight years earlier. Although honorable and necessary work, it was a setback, and I did not relish the thought of two more years of riding bumpy trails in a Jeep searching for human tracks before I became eligible again for a transfer or promotion.

2. Years later, I learned from one of their contemporaries that they had draft deferments during WWII as they were assigned to guard German POWs in camps run by the US Border Patrol. They resented the servicemen who returned from overseas at the end of the war to reclaim their jobs.

On Friday, the INS personnel office called and asked if I would take a job at the San Francisco office as a criminal investigator. I was heartened that someone there was having second thoughts, even though I would not get my job back in the border patrol. Details were being worked out, the caller said, and I should report to the INS district office in San Francisco on Monday, the day my reinstatement rights were due to expire. I made arrangements to stay at the Francis Scott Key for the weekend and rebooked my flight to Bakersfield through San Francisco.

But when I arrived at the San Francisco district office, nobody had heard of me. I waited in an outer office while phone calls were made. There had been a change of plans, I was told. Call the regional office in San Pedro later in the week.

Dominica picked me up at the airport in Bakersfield, and before going home, I had her drive me to the border patrol station. I called Mike Fargione, the INS Southwestern Region associate commissioner for enforcement, the only man I knew there. I had met him when he came to Bakersfield during the Grape Strike.

"Mr. Fargione, they're messing with me!" I blurted when he came on the line. I explained my situation in a tumble of words, pausing only when I became aware that he already knew of my predicament.

"Calm down, Mike," Fargione said soothingly. "I know it's been a long time since you've seen your family. You go home and get yourself reacquainted again, and I'll take care of getting you reinstated. I'll call you in two weeks. In the meantime, you'll be on the clock."

Being home again with my family was joyful enough to take my mind off battling the border patrol. On Saturday night, we had all our old friends over, a bring-your-own-bottle, bring-your-own-meat-to-grill blowout as we had often had before I had left, but now with amplified rock music on the new stereo I had bought in Hong Kong at Christmas time. For the party, I moved the speakers out on our patio. The celebration roared until long after midnight. We got away with it that night, but the following Saturday night, when we did it again, a neighbor on the next street over called the cops.

Mr. Fargione was as good as his word, and I was reinstated in the INS as a criminal investigator at the district office in San Francisco. I went back to work at the same grade level and with the same benefits as I would have had if I had stayed in the border patrol. It offered no recognition of my experience and time in Vietnam, but I was satisfied to be home and have a job. The government paid our moving expenses.

27

IT HAD NEVER BEEN IN ANY OF OUR PLANS or dreams, but we were excited about living in San Francisco. With the help of a realtor, Dominica found an eight-room, second-floor flat we could afford on Arguello Avenue, between the back gate of the Presidio and Golden Gate Park, and we quickly settled in.

Madison Elementary School was just around the corner on Sacramento Street, on the edge of Pacific Heights, and the girls could walk to school. But when Dominica enrolled them, we learned that Katie, an incoming third grader, would be bused to a school in the outer Richmond district as part of a pilot-busing program. Even that did not diminish our enthusiasm.

When school started in September, Dominica and I marveled at the reports of school outings: walking across the Golden Gate Bridge, visiting the Exploratorium or the De Young Museum. Before dinner each evening, the girls sat at the dining room table enthusiastically doing their homework.

I went back to school too, enrolling in night law classes at Golden Gate University School of Law on Mission Street. I attended classes from seven to ten p.m. Squeezing a full year's courses into four three-hour nights and studying on weekends cut into my precious time with the girls, but we were looking to the future.

Four young women from Rochester, New York, rented the flat downstairs. Three of them attended Catholic Lone Mountain College. The fourth, Mollie Katzen, was an aspiring artist and attended San

Francisco Art Institute.[1] Their flat became the locus of an artist, student, and musician commune that at times ranged up to a dozen youths, including, at one point, four AWOL sailors from the aircraft carrier *John Hancock*.

The kids downstairs were suspicious of me at first as being a "narc," but Dominica's gregariousness soon meant that visits up and down the back steps were commonplace. They consumed cheap red wine by the gallon jug, but we were concerned most by the pot. Early on, we secured their promise not to light up in front of our girls, and when a newcomer did, Dominica hurriedly took our girls back up the steps.

"Your daughters are going to smoke pot someday," the girls said.

"Our girls may not adopt your generation's values any more than you accepted the values of your parents," we countered. "In the meantime, they're still kids, and until they grow up, they need the love and security afforded by ours." It proved a winning argument, and we cemented friendships that lasted for many years.

We invited the kids up for our Christmas Eve, and following the reading of the Christmas story from the Bible, we exchanged gifts. Mollie, who was Jewish and had never participated in a Christmas celebration before, gave each of us a hand-painted, watercolor card featuring bouffant, pastel-colored angels and clouds.

My duties as a criminal investigator were much the same as those I had while in the patrol at Bakersfield before I had left for Vietnam. That was okay for now; we were happy being in San Francisco, happy that I had at least landed on my feet, but still wanting to get ahead.

My job involved searching for and arresting illegal immigrants, and I reported for work each morning at 6:30 a.m. at the district office on Sansome Street on the edge of Chinatown and the Financial District. I most often worked with Harry Hong, a Chinese-American born in San Francisco. With Harry as a guide, I quickly learned my way around San Francisco. Harry, his wife, Hazel, Dominica, and I often got together, frequenting the restaurants and bars of Chinatown.

I also enjoyed working with Dale Sparr, who had been middleweight champion of the Pacific Fleet during WWII and a well-known boxer in Oakland after the war. People often recognized Dale as we

1. Mollie went on to author a series of vegetarian cookbooks based on the dishes she prepared at her restaurant, the Moosewood Lodge.

worked the streets of Oakland, stopping their cars and crossing the street to shake his hand and say hello.

Dale loved to track Greek crewmen who had jumped ship in the port of San Francisco or across the bay in Oakland. At times, he got so into the chase, following one lead to the next, that we would work all day and long into the night. He had a grip like a vise, and when he grabbed the absconded sailor by the arm or shoulder, the man simply went limp, ceasing any resistance.

I reunited with Paul McClatchey, a friend and classmate from my Border Patrol Academy class in Port Isabel, Texas, and we joked about our pursuits and arrests, giving each a whimsical name. In the Barrister Bowman caper, Paul and I arrested a Canadian lawyer who had fled Canada with six million dollars of retirement savings from his clients, who were mostly widows.

The Doc Stewart caper involved a Canadian doctor the Royal Canadian Mounted Police suspected of six murders in British Columbia. Before fleeing to San Francisco, he had slain the winter caretaker at a remote church camp on Vancouver Island with a .44 Magnum rifle and, using an axe, had cut out the youth's lung to retrieve the bullet. He was believed to still be in possession of the rifle. For months Paul, Harry, and I had tracked him, but we always seemed to be one step behind. Finally, one morning, Harry and I caught up with him in a San Francisco apartment building,

The doctor knew he was cornered, but he barricaded the door. He was too clever to want to die in a shootout, I figured. He had a young woman with him who was most likely innocent of anything. Something else was up. I had learned in Vietnam to trust my instincts and never to hesitate. Gun drawn, I broke in through an unlocked window from the fire escape while Harry covered me.

I pushed open the kitchen door. The room was filled with gas; the girl was on her hands and knees, the doctor bent over her forcing her head into the oven.

"You've got to have a warrant to be in here," the doctor said with such calmness it sent a chill through me. Dignified, silver haired, he could have played a double for Robert Young, avuncular TV doctor Marcus Welby, MD. "Do you have a warrant?"

He released his grip on the slender, dark-haired girl, and she slumped unconscious to the floor. He didn't resist as I quickly handcuffed him, and watched coldly as I tried unsuccessfully to revive her.

The next morning, four RCMP officers arrived from Vancouver to take the doctor back to Canada. I picked them up at the airport, and we went to San Francisco General to interview the girl. Her parents, Italian immigrants in Canada, had arrived the previous night and were with her. She was awake but still groggy.

"Why did you save me?" she asked. "Why didn't you let me die?"

"People care for you, you know," I said, giving her the flowers Dominica had sent along with me. "My family and I are praying for you."

She smiled.

The Doc Stewart caper got Harry and me international press coverage and a trip to the trial in Canada as guests of Her Majesty the Queen.

As friendships developed with my work partners, I found myself wanting to share my experiences in Vietnam. Several of the older officers were veterans of WWII and Korea, but they seemed uninterested in the continuing war. One even questioned the capabilities and fortitude of the men who fought there. Around the coffee table or driving along in a car, conversation gravitated to anecdotes about the droll, the comedic, and sometimes the tragic events we encountered in our day-to-day work.

"The South Vietnamese Army is striking into southern Laos to cut the Ho Chi Minh Trail," I announced one morning at the coffee table, referring to the second-page story in the *Chronicle* that morning. "No American ground troops are accompanying them."

"They should have done that years ago," Harry said.

"Hope they can do it," Paul added. Then the topic turned to the team the San Francisco Giants was going to field that spring.

Other than politely acknowledging that I had been in the war, very few of our social acquaintances wanted to have a conversation about Vietnam. I wanted neither sympathy nor to be viewed as a bore, so I mostly shut up about it. Returning military veterans had VFW and American Legion clubs to go to and share experiences, but not having served in the armed services during a time of war, I was ineligible to join either organization. My service in the army had been during peacetime, 1955 to 1960, after Korea and before Vietnam.

As if my isolation was not enough, I received a letter one day from the Department of State. It instructed me to surrender the two medals I had received from the South Vietnamese government: the National Police Medal of Honor, Second Class, which I had received on my departure from Vietnam, and the Third Class Medal of Honor I had received after leaving Tam Ky.

The Foreign Decorations Act and Article 9 of the Constitution prohibit an officer or employee of the United States from accepting "any present, office, Emolument or Title, of any kind whatever, from any King, Prince, or foreign State," the letter said. I was obliged to surrender the medals and citations to the State Department for destruction. With no one to talk to and, now, not even a medal that I could legitimately hang on my wall, it was as if the country and the times were intent on squeezing my Vietnam experience out of me.

It was not easy for me to follow news about the war in the press and on TV, whose reporters and editors more often selected stories about American military failures than South Vietnamese successes. The accepted narrative about the war, that at best it was a mistake if not an example of American imperialism, had been generated by journalists skeptical about the use of American power and embraced by a generation that no longer saw military service as a duty. That view was equally widespread in literature and motion pictures.

While in Washington, DC, I had seen the new movie *M*A*S*H*. I didn't like it, feeling that it trivialized the efforts of Americans who fought in Korea. It turned out to be the least objectionable of the flood of movies depicting the blood and gore of the war, culminating in Francis Ford Coppola's *Apocalypse Now*, Oliver Stone's *Platoon*, and the seemingly endless series of *Rambo* movies.

One evening, Dominica and I walked a couple of blocks down Sacramento Street to the neighborhood theatre to see a movie. I became so enraged at the antiwar theme that I got up and walked out. Dominica followed, and we walked home in silence. I vowed never again to read a book about Vietnam written by an author of my generation and never again to view a movie about Vietnam. I was convinced that one day a history written by an author in a future generation, a historian with no emotional stake in the war, would show that our involvement there had been selfless.

Too often, the press, instead of digging out the truth, contented itself with simply casting doubt on what American and Vietnamese officials had to say, making that instead the story. I cherished memories of the people whom I had met and worked with in Vietnam: Hoang, Mui, Commissioner Toan, Chief Vinh, and the fatherly Mr. Thieu. I thought of them frequently and of all the Vietnamese men and women who were giving so much of their lives, fortunes, and dreams in the cause of a free and stable democracy of their own, the Republic of South Vietnam, and Americans who, like me, interrupted their own lives to help them. These were people the American press never seemed to discover, let alone acknowledge. More than once, in background stories about Vietnamese people and institutions, I felt from my experiences that the writer had been duped, the storyline seeming to parallel the narrative promoted by the Communist north.[2]

But in a small American Orthodox congregation that met in the chapel of a Jesuit high school in Concord, I found people with whom I could comfortably relate about the war. Dominica and I learned about the congregation when we attended a wedding in Cupertino, a very attractive ceremony in an Eastern Orthodox church. We found ourselves drawn by the Eastern Church's philosophy that God loves us, making us like him and blessing us with a free will. Because we were created in his image and likeness, we had worth.

The congregants in Concord were Russian refugees, tsarists who had fled the Soviet Union through Harbin, China, and Eastern Europeans and Poles who had fled as the Iron Curtain descended across Europe. They admired my having fought against the Communists in South Vietnam. The following spring, although I had not sought the position, I was elected treasurer of the church.

But even in church, it was impossible to wall myself from the tenor of times. The pastor, who was younger than I and like me raised an Irish Catholic, bragged openly about converting to the Orthodox faith and becoming a priest to avoid the draft and being sent to Vietnam.

2. After the war, Pham Xuam An, a Vietnamese journalist in Saigon who worked variously for *Time*, *Reuters*, and the *New York Herald Tribune* and was often relied on by American journalists for background, was awarded the retirement pay of a North Vietnamese general for his service as a spy during the war.

28

NOT ANTICIPATING LIVING IN SAN FRANCISCO, I had ordered a new car through the State Department Post Exchange catalog, a 1970 Ford Mach I. The sleek, blue muscle car had white leather upholstery, four-on-the-floor, and a 351 cubic-inch V-8 engine, a perfect fit for the broad streets and highways of Bakersfield and the culture of the valley town.

But San Francisco was decidedly different in both geography and culture. Driving down Sacramento Street to work, down over Nob Hill, through the clogged streets of Chinatown, every intersection and change of grade required manually shifting between the two lowest of the car's four gears, never reaching third.

At first, the girls were thrilled cruising with Daddy and Mommy on weekend jaunts in the shiny new sports car through wine country or along the coast. But cramped into the rear seat and taking turns accommodating a squiggly puppy on their laps, trips of any distance soon were out of the question.

Returning to the city from a drive through Napa Valley one Sunday afternoon, we came to a welcome halt at a stoplight in San Rafael. The girls were restless, and I looked for a place for ice cream or a cold drink, but we were stopped next to a used car lot. The girls were quick to spot the strange little van, the vinyl-booted spare tire mounted jauntily on the vertical front panel, the raised top flashing a wedge of orange canvas, and the sliding side door invitingly open.

"Can we stop and look at it?" Dominica asked, aware that three pairs of eyes in the back seat were longingly riveted on it. She sensed that the ungainly vehicle might afford some sort of possibility for us, if only to justify a break from the long ride.

The little van was a Volkswagen camper, we learned. If not pretty, it appeared accommodating. After a quick inspection, Katie claimed the single, rear-facing seat behind the driver while Miki and Shelly explored the back. It had a fold-down table between the bench seat in the back and the rear-facing seat behind the driver. Behind the front passenger seat was a small icebox for food and drinks. A small stainless-steel sink was built into a worktop above it, and a pump-action faucet provided water from a reservoir. There was no place to cook, but when the side door was open, a fold-up shelf could support a two-burner Coleman stove.

The back of the bench seat lowered to make a bed that extended over the rear engine compartment. The roof was hinged, and when the rear portion was raised, a canvas hammock could be opened out, which was claimed by Miki. A second hammock, stowed in the side closet, mounted to brackets on the doorposts over the bucket seats in front. Shelly laid dibs on it.

Dominica pointed out that the space on the floor under the lip of the folded down bench seat made a cozy sleeping den. Katie quickly claimed it, and her mother volunteered to cut down a pad of green foam for a mattress.

Aware that we stood to lose a lot of money by trading the four-month old Mach I so soon, I delayed committing, but it was clear that a decision had been made. By the time we crossed the Golden Gate Bridge, I had acquiesced. On Tuesday after work, I went back to the dealership and arranged to trade the shiny, new Mach I for the two-year-old Volkswagen.

Squat, boxy, her paint a lifeless shade of putty, the little camper van we dubbed Bessie played an incalculable role in mending the bonds between Dominica and me, and reuniting Miki, Shelly, and Katie with their long-absent father. Bouncing jauntily along California roads and highways, in itself an adventure, cuddling up in her interior on star-filled nights, the roar of the surf crashing in the background, our family rebuilt itself, and in doing so helped ease my transition home.

Bessie could make fifty-five miles per hour on a straight and level road, provided the wind was behind her. Her loads were heavy, but with little complaint, she carried our family and our miniature dachshund, Gretchen, to state beaches and campgrounds within a three-hundred-mile radius of our new home in San Francisco. Her load included camping gear and enough food and drink, kept cool by a ten-pound chunk of ice, for the weekend.

On Friday nights after I got home from my law classes, we packed Bessie and despite the late hour drove down the coast. Because Shelly got so tickled each time she saw the name of the street, we crossed over to Pacifica and Highway 1 on Hickey Boulevard. We often pulled off the highway at Montara Point, setting up camp in the dark on the bluff overlooking the ocean.

It was not a state campground, and there were no public facilities. We packed along an aluminum folding table and a gas lantern. Dominica prepared most meals in advance, making spaghetti sauce, stews, and casseroles at home and storing them in Ziploc bags that had only to be reheated in a pot of boiling water. The icebox kept our food, sandwich fixings, and drinks cold for a day or two before the ice had to be replenished.

The girls played on the beach with Gretchen, challenging the cold surf that lapped at their ankles but bowled over the short-legged puppy. When their jeans and tops got wet and their lips turned blue, they retreated to Bessie to change into dry clothes. I had plenty of time to read my law.

29

WHEN SUMMER CAME AND SCHOOL WAS OUT for the girls and me, we embarked on a family odyssey, a cross-country trip to visit my parents in Wisconsin whom we had not seen since 1967, a year before I left for Vietnam. We packed our star charts, which had guided a favorite activity on our camping trips on California beaches, and a large, landform map of the United States Katie had glued on poster board. Shelly brought along a *Sunset* magazine that featured an article about trilobites that could be found on a mountaintop in southern Utah. We packed a blanket and bowl for Gretchen. The girls wore their prized Oshkosh B'gosh striped bib overalls.

The first night, we stopped in Elko, Nevada. On the other side of the railroad tracks, in an old, redbrick hotel, we found the Basque restaurant we had visited on a previous trip east. The high-ceilinged dining room was well lit, and we found places at a long, communal table beside old Basque shepherds, now retired, who lived in the rooms upstairs, and local ranchers and their families.

Our tablemates passed bread and a carafe of red wine. Dominica ladled out bowls of minestrone soup from a tureen, while a waitress brought the girls tall glasses of cold milk. A large serving bowl of fresh, green salad appeared and another of red beans, followed by hush puppies and French-fried potatoes, and finally, a platter of thick steaks.

"How have you lived so long?" I asked a wiry, old Basque sitting across from me who in conversation with the girls revealed that he was ninety-nine years old.

"I always kept good habits," he said, looking at Miki, Shelly, and Katie. "I never smoked and never drank." Then turning to Dominica and me, he said, "Except every night I had one glass of red wine."

The next day, while Dominica drove, we passed around the southern end of the Great Salt Lake, and in the back, I played Mille Bornes with the girls and lunched on leftover steak. We followed two-lane US Route 40 paralleling the southern edge of the Uintah Range through eastern Utah. In the afternoon, while there was still enough light to swim, we pulled off on the grassy bank of the Duchesne River and made camp. Dominica boiled sweet corn we had picked up at a roadside stand earlier in the day. After dark, we roasted marshmallows around the campfire and broke out the star charts.

Before we turned in, I told some of the Vietnamese folk tales the girls never tired of hearing: the legend of the princess who went off to live on the moon and the forlorn prince, her lover, who organized his subjects into a procession of lights so she could find her way back. Their favorite was the story of the magic black pearl that enabled Truong, the unlucky hunter, to talk to the animals until one day it fell out of his mouth and was lost on the bottom of the sea.

The next day crossing Colorado, we turned off the highway and labored up a secondary road over the crest of the Rockies, crossing the Continental Divide at 12,500 feet. Bessie was winded but valiantly chugged on. The road was above the tree line, narrow, and winding. The surrounding terrain dropped away steeply, triggering my agoraphobia to the point I had to ask Dominica to drive. We descended through thick pine forests, the road paralleling Big Thompson Creek, finally stopping to camp for the night on the banks of the rushing stream.

Eastern Colorado was treeless and flat, and we eventually joined Interstate 80 in Nebraska. The day was hot, and the afternoon was beginning to seem endless. The four-lane interstate was straight, level, seemingly never to end. A headwind held Bessie back as if a giant hand was pushing against her broad, vertical front. We were barely making fifty miles an hour until I discovered I could draft behind eighteen-wheelers, improving our speed to just over sixty.

The prairie was blanketed with an endless carpet of wheat. The vastness of it, silent except for the rush of the wind, appeared to dwarf all human activity. The occasional colonies of farm buildings and the small towns seemed settled, normal, timeless, and impervious to political trend or change. How different it was, I reflected, from the hurly-burly of San Francisco, where new causes popped up almost daily and protests against the Vietnam war were a weekly occurrence. Violent acts such as bank robberies and power station bombings by extremist groups like the Weather Underground often made the front pages of the *San Francisco Chronicle*.

I flashed back a year to the dark hours of my second night home from Vietnam: sitting on the floor of my hotel room in Washington, DC, the room alight from the hellish, orange flames of burning cars on the street below my windows, my nostrils filled with the scent of the tear gas used by police against mobs of rioting students and that had felled me, too. I could not imagine students rioting in the bucolic settings of the towns we passed on the prairie, an insurgency taking root in this prosperous agrarian region, least of all a rebellion. It could not happen here.

This country must be like the steppes of Russia that swallowed up Napoleon's and Hitler's invading armies in their vastness, I marveled. My anger over the war and my doubts over the direction of the country seemed to disappear, too. Our nation would survive its internal fight over Vietnam, I concluded. It was just too vast, too stable, not to. I savored the thought through the remainder of the long afternoon.

A gently rolling land of giant, square cornfields, Iowa didn't easily permit travel diagonally across the state. Consequently, we stair-stepped our way to the northeast corner on back roads, past thousands of acres of corn, and along the main streets of neatly arranged, small towns.

In mid-afternoon, we reached Dubuque, passing in reverent awe under arches formed by stately elms, their upswept branches meeting over the street like the ceiling of a cathedral. We crossed the Mississippi on a two-lane, truss bridge and chugged to the top of the bluff.

A stoutly built farmer stood at the side of a green, John Deere tractor at the near edge of a field, a patch of red, flannel underwear exposed at his waist where his striped Oshkosh B'gosh overalls could not come together. Pressing a pudgy finger to the side of his nose, he cleared each of his nostrils into the wind.

"E-yew!" the girls and Dominica exclaimed in unison. Their Oshkoshes, the envy of their classmates at Madison School in San Francisco, were thrown in the wash that night and never worn again.

In the lengthening sunlight of late afternoon, we wound our way on narrow roads through lush, Kelly-green valleys cradled by steep, tree-covered hills, inhaling the rich scent of newly turned, black soil. My mother often said our Irish ancestors had settled in this place because it reminded them so much of Ireland. This was my home turf, Southwestern Wisconsin, the prosperous looking fields of growing hay, newly planted corn, and green meadows dotted with pasturing milk cows.

We arrived in Richland Center in early evening. My parents and my sister Anne still lived in the flat above a downtown store that had once been our grocery store. Dad had been forced out of business by the arrival of the new Piggly Wiggly but now sold advertising novelties: pens, calendars, key cases, note pads. Incredibly, he was making more money at it than he ever had in the grocery business.

We clumped up the long, dark flight of stairs and were welcomed at the top by my mother. Dad stood with his hands on his hips, beaming. It had been four years since my parents had seen their grandchildren, and there were joyful hugs and surprises all around.

A midwestern homecoming required a picnic, and Mom organized it at Krouskop Park. Anne was getting married that weekend, and my twin brother, Pat, and his wife, Marilyn, drove up from Chicago with their two children. My sister Mary, her husband, Ron, and their three children came over from nearby Prairie du Sac. The cousins were all slightly younger, but not so much that they and the girls couldn't be good playmates. The girls kept their Oshkoshes out of sight.

My younger brother, Tim, after a two-year stint in the army, including a year in Germany, was home and working for Greyhound in Madison. He had been sent to Germany because army policy prohibited brothers from simultaneously serving in a war zone.

The day of Anne's wedding was as humid and hot as only the upper Midwest could be. She was just seven when I had left home for the army sixteen years earlier, and with the exception of the year and a half I had attended the University of Wisconsin, we had seen each other only infrequently since. Suddenly, she was a married woman.

Early on the morning after the wedding, we packed into Bessie for the trip home.

The sun was setting when on the second evening we pulled off the interstate at Wamsutter, a tiny rural town in central Wyoming. Our landform map said we were in the Great Divide Basin. Looking for a suitable place to camp for the night, we drove a mile or so past the village limits on a dirt road. When it played out, we stopped on the boundary-less plain under a wide-open sky.

As a boy, I dreamed of camping out west in Wyoming, but Dad didn't drive, and we didn't own a car. Now, I was finally experiencing it with a family of my own. We built our campfire that night under the stars and told stories until late.

We left early the next morning, and Shelly dug out the *Sunset* magazine containing the article about trilobites. Following the directions in the article, we left I-80 and toddled along a lonely two-lane highway through central Utah. Thirty miles southwest of Delta, we turned off on an unmarked dirt road and drove thirty more miles through barren scrubland up into a range of low mountains. Eventually, the road simply petered out in the sparse grass at the rim of a broad canyon.

We piled out of Bessie and found ourselves completely alone; there were no buildings, signs, or fences. Only a few, faint tire tracks indicated that others had been there before us. We walked to the rim of the canyon and, overpowered by the silence, stood in awe of the broad expanse of unspoiled western vista. No sign of human habitation was visible. I looked back at Bessie. Her squat, metal, and glass body, standing alone on the scrub grass, looked like a putty-colored spaceship stranded on an alien planet.

A dozen or so feet down the steep slope, a dark band, as level as a contour line on a map, extended along the wall of the canyon as far as we could see. The *Sunset* article said it was the shoreline of an ancient sea, and that added wonder to our view. Five hundred million years later, this prehistoric beach rimmed the top of a mountain 6,500 feet above sea level, hundreds of miles from the Pacific Ocean, two and a half states away.

We clambered down the slope to the band of dark shale. We were able to break it apart in our hands into flat, wafer-life slabs.

With no effort at all, we snapped out our first trilobite, preserved like a leaf pressed between the pages of an old book. The oblong exoskeleton, about an inch in length, had a head, three parallel courses of ribs, and a tail.

As we bent to our task, the immense silence of this lonely mountaintop was broken by the snap of brittle wafers of shale. We popped out trilobites as if we were shelling peanuts, irreverently exposing the fossilized shells of creatures that until this moment had lain buried in layers of silt for a half a billion years. We were discovering Genesis first-hand, and we felt the presence of God.

In a whimsical moment, I calculated that my time on Earth was 33/500,000,000 of the age of the trilobite fossils. The span of our lives was a mere instant on an Earth billions of years old.

Vietnamese civilization extended so far back that I had often thought our involvement there would one day rate but one or two lines in the thousands of verses of their creation story, but even that reflection was now forced into a much broader perspective. The war that preoccupied so much of my time and thought, in fact the entire epic of the Vietnamese people, was the tiniest instant in the history of the world.

On the plains and prairies of Colorado and Nebraska, I had discovered the stabilizing power of mid-America. On this ancient beach, I discovered the relevance of time. Humans were as much a part of the time/space environment so evident on this half-billion-year-old shoreline as the trilobites, but there was something more; we humans had evolved, even developing to the point we could change our environment. How was that so, I wondered? Whatever the answer to that, I felt ever more deeply my responsibility to my fellow man and the world we inhabited, if only for so short a time.

That evening, we built a campfire, roasted marshmallows, and made s'mores. We talked about the Earth, about God and creation, and looked with more wonder than ever at the stars.

We started early the next morning, our last day on the road, and through the long afternoon, we bumped across a seemingly endless series of dry basins and low mountain ranges. The sun set as we climbed the east slope of the Sierras. Everyone else was asleep when we crossed the Bay Bridge, leaving me alone to marvel at the lights of the new skyscrapers in the Financial District and the more familiar glow of Chinatown and Nob Hill. We arrived home after ten p.m. and stumbled up the stairs to our flat, lugging only the bedding we would need for the night. We were tired and had little left to say.

I had found a new assurance on our journey, a renewed confidence in America, and the capability of humans to get it right over time. The importance I had attached to the Vietnam War and the antiwar protests faded against the backdrop of America's heartland and the realization of the time continuum on which we lived. Our country was immense enough to accommodate it all.

30

In the spring of 1973, President Nixon sent a bill to Congress to consolidate the resources of all federal agencies charged with enforcing narcotics laws into a new federal agency, the Drug Enforcement Administration. Among the organizations slated to lose personnel or be entirely absorbed into the DEA, the Customs Service was required to transfer all its drug investigators to the new agency. To assuage the politically powerful agency and its congressional supporters—port directors of Customs were still patronage jobs and jealous of their domains—the INS would be required to transfer its immigration inspectors working at air, land, and sea ports of entry to Customs. The INS stood to lose its presence at ports of entry and 15 percent of its workforce in the new arrangement. Enforcement against illegal entry on the Mexican border would be bifurcated between not just two federal agencies but also two cabinet departments.

Soon after arriving in San Francisco, I had been elected president of our union lodge, Local 1616, American Federation of Government Employees, AFL-CIO. I was not directly affected by the reorganization, but the office was slated to lose its large staff of airport and seaport inspectors. The employees believed in the importance of their jobs, and to a person they did not want to go to the Customs Service where they felt their skills and training would no longer be valued.

"Presidential Reorganization Plan No. 2 of 1973 has been sent to Congress," the president of the National INS Council, the umbrella organization for all INS locals warned me when I called. "If neither House of Congress passes a resolution opposing it within the next sixty days, it becomes law. It would be futile, if not impossible, for us to oppose it.

"The administration is promising that customs inspectors, which will mean our guys, too, will be given an upgrade and have more lucrative overtime pay," the council president said. "We're gonna take the deal."

Despite the possibility of higher pay, the immigration inspectors at San Francisco rejected the offer. An entirely different culture existed in the Customs Service whose charge at ports of entry was to assess and collect duty and prevent the entry of contraband. Immigration inspectors, on the other hand, determined the eligibility of arriving people to enter the United States and, if a non-citizen or immigrant, the conditions he or she must abide if admitted or paroled.

All INS officers began their careers serving at least two years in the US Border Patrol on the Mexican border before becoming eligible for promotion to immigration inspector at a port of entry. Their one-year training program included sixteen weeks of immigration law and Spanish at the US Border Patrol Academy in Port Isabel, Texas. Written examinations in immigration law and oral boards in Spanish at the end of five and a half months and again at ten months determined if an officer would be retained or dismissed.

The US Customs Service, on the other hand, provided only eight weeks of formal training, and frequently it was not in a formal setting but on the job. Customs employees were not required to speak Spanish, an essential skill for enforcing immigration laws. Transferring 1,500 trained, Spanish-speaking immigration officers to the Customs Service would be a huge loss to the INS and, at a time when it was severely pressed on the Mexican border, greatly diminish its ability to prevent illegal entry.

If our union local in San Francisco wanted to defy its national leadership and try to defeat the president's reorganization plan, we'd have to do it alone. I was up for the challenge.

I called the House Government Operations Committee and learned that a hearing on the reorganization plan was scheduled for the following week, but no one had registered as a witness in opposition to the bill. I explained that I was a local union president and asked if I could appear.

"Yes, of course," the committee staff director said. "We'd like to hear an opposing view."

The local voted to pay for my round-trip ticket on the red-eye flight to Washington, DC, and reimburse me for three days' expenses. I had less than a week to prepare, but after work each day, members pitched in to compile statistics and data on the unprecedented surge of legal and illegal immigration over the past seven years and its impact on our office and the area we served, Northern California and Nevada.

Alarmed by the potential reduction of already short services—the newly liberalized Immigration and Nationality Act meant a more than doubling of arrivals of new immigrants—members of the Bay Area Immigration Bar Association gave me letters of introduction to the chairman of the Government Operations Committee, Chet Holifield, and other influential congressmen, including Carl Albert, the Speaker of the House. Immigrant aid organizations made appointments for me at their national offices to talk to their legislative affairs staffs. To make sure I could see my congressman in his office in Washington, DC, I dropped by his local office and gave him a fifty-dollar campaign contribution.

At the hearing, members of Congress who had never heard of illegal immigrants, and knew little or nothing about the increasing numbers of legal immigrants and travelers to the United States, interrupted me often with questions. It took over two hours for me to get through my prepared statement.

"Border patrol apprehensions on the Mexican border have increased from forty-four thousand in 1964 to almost a million in 1972 while our resources have remained static," I testified, using statistics never before revealed to Congress. The administration maintained that the INS was "providing an acceptable level of enforcement" on the Mexican border.

"Outnumbered border patrol agents in the Chula Vista sector who have a group of a dozen illegal border crossers in custody often are forced to watch helplessly as a group of thirty or forty more trot past them not fifty yards away," I related. "Drug smugglers are recruiting or extorting the border crossers into muling drugs. If we can't stop the people who carry them, we can't stop the drugs." The point hit home because the surge of drugs hitting the streets of American cities was the underlying reason for creating the DEA.

"The Customs Service makes little use of its inspectors' down time between arrivals and during low-volume midnight shifts," I said, seeking to deliver a *coup de grâce*. "During slow periods at ports of entry and to fill out their eight-hour shifts, immigration inspectors adjudicate visa petitions filed by your constituents to bring their parents, spouses, brothers, and sisters to the United States. If immigration inspectors are transferred to the Customs Service, the INS will lose over seven hundred thousand hours of their productivity, which will have to be replaced or absorbed by longer wait times for your constituents." On the dais, every eye was on me.

During the day, I walked the halls of the House office buildings and visited the offices of voluntary agencies and labor unions to encourage them to support us. Each evening in my room at the Burlington Hotel, I ordered a grilled ham-and-cheese sandwich and two bottles of Michelob from room service and got on the phone.

I called fellow union officers at INS offices, ports of entry, and border patrol stations across the country. They arranged additional appointments for me with their home-district member of Congress and wrote letters. Money to keep me in Washington started rolling in. My supervisors in San Francisco, as concerned about the impact of the reorganization plan on the INS as were their employees, were quick to approve my weekly requests for additional vacation time.

The Government Operations Subcommittee was scheduled to vote on a resolution to disapprove the reorg plan the following week, and late in the afternoon the day before, I counted it two votes shy of passage. I went to see Texas congressman and House majority leader Jim Wright.

"I'm not going to be there tomorrow, but I'll give my vote to another member. "Whom do you want me to give it to?" Wright asked after hearing me out.

"Give it to Chairman Holifield," I said. The chairman was from southern California and knew first-hand the impact of the surge in legal and illegal immigration in the state.

At the end of the roll call the next morning, the motion to disapprove was passing by one vote. It was time for the chairman to vote.

Congressman Holifield picked up his gavel and looked me straight in the eye. "The chair votes Mr. Wright, nay. And himself, nay."

I slumped in my seat, thinking I had failed. The chairman called for the next vote, one to bind the motion to disapprove over to the full committee. This time, he voted himself and Mr. Wright aye. It took a minute to digest what he had done, but then I realized the motion was still alive, to be voted on again the following week.

Elated, that night from the Burlington, I spread the news. We had won an initial victory. In a week's time, we had the votes of fifteen more members to obtain, and that night I got to work. But even with Chairman Holifield and Mr. Wright's vote, the full committee split 15-15, putting the decision over yet another week.

I had pushed aside the equivocating leadership of the INS Council but gotten the cooperation of our parent, the AFGE. Viewing the influx of illegal, cheap labor with increasing concern, the AFL-CIO now weighed in beside us, as did the national immigrant services organizations and veterans groups I had spent time recruiting. With their support on the hill, we won the next vote hands down. The motion to disapprove would now go to a floor vote in the House of Representatives, and it appeared likely to pass

The following day, a request to meet was relayed to me from the director of the White House, Office of Management and Budget. The meeting was held in a conference room at the International Inn on Thomas Circle on the Saturday afternoon of Memorial Day weekend, I brought along a dozen INS and border patrol employees who had come to Washington, DC, when they could to visit offices on Capitol Hill. I sat at the table with AFGE president Clyde Weber and AFL-CIO general counsel Ken Meiklejohn. Fred Malek, deputy director of the Office of Management and Budget, dressed in slacks and a casual sweater as if he had broken away from a weekend barbeque, sat across from us.[1]

"What do you guys want?" Malek asked with a sweep of his arm, avoiding looking at us.

"We want immigration inspectors and their work to remain with the INS," AFGE President Weber said.

1. Malek was the author of the Nixon-era *Malek Manual: How to Fire Federal Employees.*

"It can't be done," Malek insisted. "The Presidential Reorganization Act does not allow for a plan submitted to Congress to be amended."

"Don't tell me it can't be done," Weber thundered, pounding his fist on the table for emphasis. "I've seen bills resurrected from the bowels of the Congress!"

Malek called for a recess and huddled with the dozen White House and agency officials who accompanied him.

When they returned, his deputy spoke. "In return for your commitment to cease opposition to Reorganization Plan No. 2 of 1973, the administration will send Congress a bill to prospectively repeal that portion of the plan that relates to the Immigration and Naturalization Service. We will support the bill and, pending its enactment, the Office of Management and Budget will hold in abeyance implementation of those portions of the plan that affect the INS."

It was an impossible, but very satisfying, grassroots victory, and I achieved overnight rock-star status in the INS, the AFL-CIO, and the myriad immigrant services agencies that supported us. I had also become a familiar figure on Capitol Hill, especially to the members and their staffs who had budget or legislative oversight of the INS. After five weeks in Washington, DC, the victory under my belt, I returned home to San Francisco and went back to work.

The OMB was as good as its word—immigration inspectors and their function stayed with the INS, but my career in the agency was forever changed. Little could I know then that my trip to Washington, DC, would be the first in a series of improbable events that five years later would take me back to Southeast Asia.

In the fall, needing to face up to our overwhelmed southern border defenses, President Nixon appointed former Marine Corps commandant, General Leonard F. Chapman to be commissioner of the INS. His predecessor had chosen to retire when the president submitted the reorganization plan to Congress, leaving the position vacant for several months, and General Chapman got right to work.

The general pressed for more personnel and equipment and a law penalizing employers for hiring illegal aliens. He went directly to the press and the public.

"The INS is being asked to carry a ten-ton load in a five-ton truck," the general said.

Commissioner Chapman brought just two people with him to the INS, public information officer Verne Jervis and research and development director Ed Scott. Recognizing the growing friction over the burgeoning population of Mexican illegal immigrants, he hired E. B. Duarte to be his director of outreach to the Hispanic community. I got along well with each of these three key members of his staff, and they and Commissioner Chapman often brought me to Washington, DC, for consultation. Because of my union office, I could conveniently go off the clock and on the union dollar deliver a message or two on Capitol Hill or to the AFL-CIO, and I often did.

At the end of a day, I often lingered with General Chapman and one or the other of his staff in his office. He probed my insights into border issues. I shared news and views I picked up in my rounds of congressional, AFL-CIO, and voluntary agency offices. He shared his plans for the INS with me, but often our conversations drifted to Vietnam. I had at last found a fellow veteran of the war to talk to, someone with whom to share my wartime experiences.

One morning, the general's legislative assistant, Neil Leary, called me at home in San Francisco. "General Chapman wants to know if you'd move to Washington and work on his staff full-time," he asked.

Dominica and I had long before decided that when the girls reached high school age, the family would stay put wherever we were. Miki had been in junior high when, faced with a five-fold increase in our rent, we moved from our flat in San Francisco to suburban Concord. The move had been tough for her; she had had her heart set on attending Galileo High School. Now, all three of our daughters were settled in high school, and we did not want to move them again.

"I'm sorry, Neil," I said. "Because of family concerns, moving to Washington is out of the question. Besides, without my position in the union, I'll lose my entrée to the AFL-CIO and wouldn't be nearly as useful to the general and the INS as I may be now."

I continued to commute to Washington, DC, at least once a month, sometimes twice.

31

As the New Year, 1975, began, alarming news from South Vietnam grabbed my attention. On January 6, Phuoc Long, a province bordering Cambodia north of Saigon, fell to the North Vietnamese Army.

When I had left South Vietnam in the late spring of 1970, many of us involved in the joint US/South Vietnamese Pacification effort had believed that despite the withdrawal of US ground troops, with continued economic aid and the support of American airpower, South Vietnam could defend itself against the North and maintain its independence. Three years later, in the spring of 1973, the North Vietnamese Army launched the Easter Offensive, invading the South across its borders. The South Vietnamese Army, unaided by US ground troops but receiving American air support, repelled them. It confirmed the hopes that many of us had for the country.

Peace talks began in earnest that fall but soon became a quagmire. After a massive US bombing campaign, including the mining of Haiphong harbor, the North signed the Paris Accords in January 1973, pledging to cease attacks and infiltration against the South. The last twenty-nine thousand US combat troops came home, along with our prisoners of war, some who had been in captivity for six or seven years. The United States stopped the bombing campaign.

Despite the treaty, North Vietnam did not cease in its attempts to take over the South by force. One hundred sixty thousand North Vietnamese troops remained in the South. At the bargaining table in Paris, the United States had ignored President Thieu's demand that, as a condition to the accords, the North Vietnamese Army leave South

Vietnam. To resupply and reinforce them, no longer hindered by US bombing, the North Vietnamese Army rebuilt the Ho Chi Minh into a paved, four-lane highway. They laid four petroleum pipelines into South Vietnam as far south as the provinces adjacent to Saigon. Immediately after the signing of the Paris Accords, the US Navy removed the mines that blockaded Haiphong Harbor. Hundreds of thousands of tons of Russian and Chinese equipment flooded down the trail from the North.

In order to get South Vietnamese President Thieu's acceptance of the Paris Accord, President Nixon and Secretary of State Henry Kissinger, in at least three side letters, pledged to come to South Vietnam's aid if the country was attacked again.

After the attack on Phuoc Long Province, the US State Department issued a strongly worded protest, but President Gerald Ford sent no B-52 bombers into the air.[1] With no US air support, the South Vietnamese Army failed to retake the province, and it stayed in Communist hands. I felt worse would soon come.

In March, twenty divisions of the North Vietnamese Army, over one hundred thousand men, invaded the Central Highlands. On March 10, 1975, three NVA divisions, outnumbering the defenders 25,000 to 1,200, defeated the garrison at Ban Me Thuot in a matter of days, unhinging the defenses of Pleiku and Kontum further north. During the Paris Talks, President Thieu had vowed to his people that his government would cede no territory to the North, but now he had little choice other than to order the two provinces abandoned.

Chaos set in; the roads filled with refugees. Further north, Quang Tri Province, Quang Ngai Province, and the cities of Hue and Danang, fell in quick succession, at a rate of almost one a day.[2]

I searched the newspapers for word of Tam Ky but found no mention of it. During the war, the American press rarely mentioned the province capital by name, referring to it only as "an area fifty miles south of Danang," but now there was not even that. Television news showed film of desperate South Vietnamese soldiers in Danang harbor trying futilely to jump from the dock to the deck of a rescue ship and being crushed against the pilings. The owner of World Airways

1. Lewis Sorley, *A Better War: The Unexamined Victories and Final Tragedy of America's Last Years in Vietnam*, New York: Harcourt (1999), 374.
2. Ibid., 377.

landed a 727 aircraft at Danang airport, hoping to establish an airlift out of the city. The plane was mobbed before it could come to a stop on the runway and took off immediately, flying to Saigon at two thousand feet with its wheels down, panicked soldiers clinging to hydraulic lines in the wheel wells.

General Chapman confirmed my fears about the fate of Tam Ky. Tien Phuoc District had been overrun on March 11. After holding out for two more weeks, Tam Ky fell. Among the units that had fought valiantly but had been overwhelmed was a battalion of the National Police Field Force. The North Vietnamese Army had finally achieved the objective, capturing Tam Ky and reaching the coast, that had cost them so dearly over so many years.

I anguished over the fate of Hoang and Mui, of Vinh and Mr. Thieu, of Mr. An and his little daughter, whom I had carried aboard the *Helgoland*. I thought of Commissioner Toan and the hundreds of police I had met in the villages we visited and the families who had shown us hospitality. Many would be executed, I feared, in brutal reprisal for their participation in the Village Police and the Phoenix Program, which had eliminated the Viet Cong infrastructure. Others faced years of confinement and hard labor in Communist reeducation camps. I feared that copies of the photos I had taken in each village, of the police lined up in front of their headquarters, would now serve to identify them to their Communist captors.

At Xuan Loc, forty miles northeast of Saigon, the South Vietnamese Army held out for a month destroying three of the attacking North Vietnamese divisions, but even I saw little hope that, without military support and more foreign aid, South Vietnam could turn the desperate tide of defeat.

Senator Edward Kennedy, the younger brother of President John F. Kennedy, who had decided to take a stand against Communist expansionism in South Vietnam, had sponsored an amendment to cut American aid to the country to one billion dollars in 1975, less than what was provided to Israel. Worldwide inflation that year, triggered by the oil crises, reduced the effective amount to $645 million. Without more aid, according to the South Vietnamese Army Chief of Staff, the country would run out of fuel in mid-May and ammunition by June.

The US advisory goal in South Vietnam was always to help the new nation get to the point where it could defend itself. The virtual elimination of the Viet Cong by 1970, progress in the pacification effort, and the success of the South Vietnamese Army in blunting the North Vietnamese Easter Offensive indicated success. The people were coalescing around their national government. In 1971, 87.7 percent of registered voters cast ballots in the national election.[3]

We had every reason to conclude that so long as the United States continued to provide logistical and financial support, South Vietnam would be able to resist aggression without the aid of US ground forces. But in the face of the new North Vietnamese invasion, the United States had not lifted a finger, reneging on its commitment to come to the aid of the country with air and sea power, cutting economic aid to the point that the South Vietnamese armed forces could no longer repair or replace equipment destroyed in battle or buy ammunition.

Ambassador Colby once said the South Vietnamese could do anything they believed they could, but it was now clear they no longer thought they could survive as an independent country. Still short of the effective leaders that in a developing country can only come through experience, many in higher-level positions began to look for ways to bail out.

In the weeks before the fall, I was often on Capitol Hill visiting congressional offices. After the business at hand had been conducted, I lingered, begging members to resume aid to South Vietnam, to send the B-52s, but to no avail.

"The war is over," one congressman said sympathetically.

"We have to end it," said another.

President Thieu resigned, disgusted at the US betrayal, and went into exile in Paris.

At Tulane University, President Ford said that as far as the United States was concerned, the war in Vietnam was finished.[4]

Tanks rolled into Saigon, having driven unimpeded down the Ho Chi Minh trail, fueled by the pipeline that now extended all the way to the outskirts of the city. Saigon fell on April 30. Americans watching their TV sets didn't notice that the wrought-iron gates of the Presidential Palace were torn down not by a popular uprising of

3. Ibid., 280.
4. Ibid., 379.

South Vietnamese peasants, as predicted by many of the pundits and journalists who were responsible for the prevailing narrative of the war, but by the tanks of the North Vietnamese Army. Viewers in the United States were riveted instead by the pictures of Americans and their Vietnamese dependents pushing to find space in a Huey on the roof of the embassy.

Many Americans drew a sigh of relief that the Vietnam War was over. Some celebrated. I felt we had pulled the plug on an ally, abandoned its people to an unknown future under Communism.

I was ashamed for my country.

32

JIMMIE CARTER WAS ELECTED PRESIDENT in 1976, and a new president meant a new direction for the INS. Carter selected a young Mexican-American politician, the comptroller of the city of Houston, Texas, Leonel Castillo, to be the head of the agency.

From the outset, the appointment of a Mexican-American to the commissioner's post met skepticism. The number of arrests by the border patrol had exploded to over one million annually, but many people, within the INS as well as congressional and media observers, took the appointment of Castillo to signal a softening of immigration enforcement rather than a crackdown. As if to prove it, his first official action was to decree that the INS would no longer refer to people who were unlawfully in the United States as "illegal aliens" but as "undocumented workers."

The new commissioner and I were both scheduled to participate in a symposium on immigration at the Center for the Study of Democratic Institutions in Santa Barbara the weekend before he took office. The afternoon before the event, he called me in San Francisco and introduced himself.

"This is Leonel Castillo, the new commissioner," he said right off the bat. "I see you're on the program tomorrow in Santa Barbara. I am, too, and I'd like to get together with you there. Are you bringing your wife? I'd like to meet her, too."

I had already planned to take Dominica, and that afternoon after work, we drove down to Santa Barbara and checked into the Biltmore, a grand, Southern California jazz-age hotel where symposium participants were being housed. We arrived at the Biltmore at about ten p.m. Mr. Castillo, a young, stocky, broad-faced man with a perpetual grin, was waiting for us in the lobby. After checking in, the three of us walked to a nearby Red Robin restaurant and found a booth in the back. We drank coffee, ate pie, and talked until 3 a.m.

Mr. Castillo and I found we had many mutual acquaintances and much to discuss. Through my frequent congressional and public appearances, I had gained a reputation as the go-to person on immigration issues. Not long into our conversation, the commissioner arrived at the point of our meeting and his reason for asking me to bring Dominica.

"None of my immediate staff has experience with immigration," Castillo said. "I'd like you to come to Washington to work with us."

It was an attractive offer, but not one I could accept. I explained why I had refused General Chapman's invitation; our daughters were in high school, and we did not want to move them.

Castillo acknowledged that for the same reason his family had decided to stay in Houston.

"Would you come on a temporary basis on government per diem?" he asked.

"President Carter wants to create a new Border Management Agency combining the resources of the Customs Service and the Immigration Service. In addition to working with me and my staff, I'd like you to be my representative on the committee that puts this together."

"I'll do it only if the INS has a fair shot at being the lead agency, and I mean combining inspectors of both agencies into the INS," I responded. I had spent too much time on the issue not to be interested, but immediately I realized that I had just made a commitment to more travel away from home. Dominica didn't object.

A series of two- and three-week stints in Washington, DC, evolved into an informal arrangement: I worked three weeks out of every month in Castillo's office in Washington, DC, and one week in my day job at the San Francisco district office. Counting weekends, I spent eleven days each month at home.

In Washington, DC, I spent a lot of time mentoring Castillo's staff and an equal amount of time trying to ease their presence into an agency that considered them outsiders. Some headquarters employees derisively called the top floor corner suite where Castillo and his staff had their offices the "Mexican corner." Suspicions traveled both ways, but over time, they began to melt.

Most members of Castillo's staff were batching it, too, and we were in the office a lot of evenings and weekends. We often walked to a nearby Chinese restaurant on H Street for dinner. Castillo was filled with ideas for building a more compassionate, more responsive Immigration and Naturalization Service. At his behest, I traveled to Los Angeles and evaluated satellite offices established in Anaheim and Long Beach, areas where most immigrants lived, instead of the downtown business cores where INS offices had been traditionally located. Then, pursuing an idea of my own that would dovetail with the satellite office concept, I flew up to Anchorage to look at a position unique to Alaska that combined both enforcement and examinations duties.

One afternoon in January, Castillo called me into his office and handed me a letter he had just received from the chair of the House Immigration Subcommittee, congressman Joshua Eilberg. Chairman Eilberg asked him to appear and testify on a bill to authorize the attorney general to parole seven thousand Vietnamese boat refugees into the United States.

"This may interest you since you were in Vietnam," Castillo said. "How about taking it on?"

The hearing was three weeks away.

In January 1978, thousands of Vietnamese refugees languished in camps established by the United Nations High Commission for Refugees along the coasts of Thailand, Malaysia, Singapore, Hong Kong, and the Philippines, with little hope of resettlement in the free world. The United States had evacuated 145,000 Vietnamese when it left the country in1975, most of whom had connections to the US war effort. Following the evacuation, the attorney general continued to use his emergency authority to parole Vietnamese who made it into the camps and could establish they had worked for the US government during the war, had been a high-level official in the Government of South Vietnam, or had a close relative that was an American citizen. Under the restrictive criteria, the number of refugees taken from the camps for resettlement in the United States slowed to a mere trickle;

fewer than three thousand were accepted over the two years following the end of the war.

The authority to resettle Southeast Asian refugees at the end of the war expired in September 1977, leaving close to seven thousand boat people stranded in the camps. A hearing on a bill to authorize the resettlement of the remaining "boat cases" was held in July, but no action on the bill ensued. Instead, Congress expressed skepticism over the continued use of the attorney general's emergency parole powers and suggested the appointment of a Joint Legislative/Executive Select Committee to study a permanent solution. A new law and resettlement of the boat people in the camps would be years off.

Following the unsatisfying end of the long, controversial war and the resignation of an American president triggered by a tawdry political crime, the mood of the country had slipped into malaise. The Bicentennial celebration in 1976 seemed an almost joyless event. Americans wanted to turn the page. No one wanted to think about refugees from Vietnam, let alone bring them to the United States. Public indifference abetted congressional inaction. As the memory of our promises to defend South Vietnam faded, it appeared the country was trying to forget the people we had pledged to help as well.

Officially, the United States viewed the boat refugees as fleeing bad economic conditions in the Socialist Republic of Vietnam and not people suffering persecution for their political beliefs. If we started bringing the boat people to the United States, some administration officials argued, the stream would become a torrent. Many Vietnamese would die, creating a humanitarian crisis on the South China Sea and the Gulf of Thailand forcing the United States to resettle a large and possibly unwelcome new population of immigrants. [1]

Based on very little evidence, an unsympathetic press speculated that the refugees were the wealthy Chinese merchant class fleeing a crackdown by the new regime, bribing and paying their way with gold. Other commentators said they were draft evaders, fleeing to

[1] With the exception of the Displaced Persons Act of 1948 and 1950, US policy towards refugees had been ad hoc, largely directed towards resettling escapees from Communist-dominated countries. The Hungarian Escape Act of 1958 authorized the parole of fifty-eight thousand "freedom fighters," after the failed Hungarian revolt. Thousands of Czechs were paroled after the Communist regime with Soviet help crushed the Prague Spring revolt. Russian Jews and Pentecostals continue to be admitted as refugees, even after the collapse of the Soviet Union. Every US president since Eisenhower has offered refuge to Cubans who could make it to US shores. The United States brought 145,000 Vietnamese with them when they abandoned the country in 1975.

avoid conscription for service in "Vietnam's Vietnam," the Socialist Republic's invasion of Cambodia to overthrow the murderous dictator, Pol Pot, or to defend the country against the invading Chinese on the northern border.

The bill to authorize the attorney general's parole of seven thousand boat people, the estimated population of the camps in July, was meant as a measured response to the crisis, but some White House and State Department officials, as well as the House Immigration subcommittee chair, believed the exodus was abating and would soon end.

Instead, the crisis was growing. Through the fall and winter, an estimated one thousand Vietnamese were arriving in Thailand, Malaysia, and Singapore each month, but most were turned away. Few made it into the overcrowded camps. By January 1978, the original estimate of seven thousand was starting to appear woefully inadequate, but in the US Congress, the boat people seemed to have no constituency.

Compelled by the slow pace of refugee resettlement by the United States and other countries, Thailand, Malaysia, and Singapore enacted laws barring further entry of refugees and began forcing refugee boats back to sea. Thailand and Singapore applied the new policy harshly. Malaysia allowed distressed refugees' boats to land but, after repairing their vessels, forced the occupants to sail on. Nobody knew the fate of the boat refugees forced back to sea, where they went, or how many perished.

American embassy and INS officials continued to periodically screen recent arrivals in the camps for former US government employees and their families who were then granted parole into the United States. The State Department and the INS officers who visited the camps, citing reports of hunger and food distribution problems in the new Socialist Republic of Vietnam, called those remaining "economic refugees" and therefore not eligible for political asylum.

I saw it differently. Even if the stories about the flight of the Chinese merchant class were true, the fishermen who owned the boats and their families were fleeing, too. There were bountiful fishing resources along the coast of Vietnam, and if fishermen were starving, it was because they were prevented from consuming their own catch or unable to trade it for rice. Rice, too, was plentiful. Even during the war, Vietnam exported much of its rice crop. It appeared that the worst fears of Vietnamese fisherman and rice farmers had come true. Hungry, deprived of their crops and catches by the collectivization of their yields by the new Communist regime, they were forced to flee.

For the Congressional hearing, I would have to gather data, facts, and the refugees' own stories. To do that, I would have to go to the camps and interview them. Pointing out that we had no first-hand information about why the boat people were leaving Vietnam to cite in his testimony before the House Committee, I persuaded Commissioner Castillo to let me go to Southeast Asia and take a look.

On a personal level, I was concerned about the people whom I had met and worked with in Vietnam. I often checked INS records to see if anyone I knew had somehow escaped and found his or her way to the United States. Only Vinh had made it out. I was haunted by the thought that I might find someone I knew in the camps. What would I say?

The United States had selflessly sent almost three million young men and women to aid the South Vietnamese during the war; fifty-eight thousand had died. Yet at Paris in secret side agreements, we betrayed them, and subsequently, despite our pledge to come to their aid if the North Vietnamese renewed their invasion, we not only refused to unleash our air and sea power; we also withdrew the military and economic aid that was their only hope for survival. As an American, I shared the guilt and was ashamed. How would the refugees look at me, or I at them?

33

On a cold and snowy Washington, DC, afternoon, I caught a flight out of Dulles to San Francisco, the first leg of my journey to Thailand to visit the camps where the boat people were detained. Dominica met me at the San Francisco airport, and I swapped my winter coat and gloves for a suitcase of summer-weight clothing. In an hour, I was on my way to Tokyo.

The next day, I checked in with the INS district director in Hong Kong, Sam Feldman, and the following afternoon arrived in Bangkok. An embassy officer with a car and driver met me. We left immediately for a refugee camp near the Cambodian border, overnighting in Pattaya, made famous during the Vietnam War as an R & R destination for American troops.

We arrived at Laem Sing, a five-acre tract of sandy beach at the base of a steep cliff where over one thousand Vietnamese and Khmer refugees were housed in a makeshift village of thatch, bamboo, and black Visqueen huts. We pulled up behind a tank truck parked on the road above the camp. Several Vietnamese toting plastic containers were bartering with a Thai driver and a helper for water. I was surprised I was still able to catch enough Vietnamese words to understand what was transpiring.

A steep trail led down to the camp. Thai police were stationed at the entrance to the site, and the camp director, Sam Hall, an American employed by the United Nations High Commission for Refugees (UNHCR), met us.

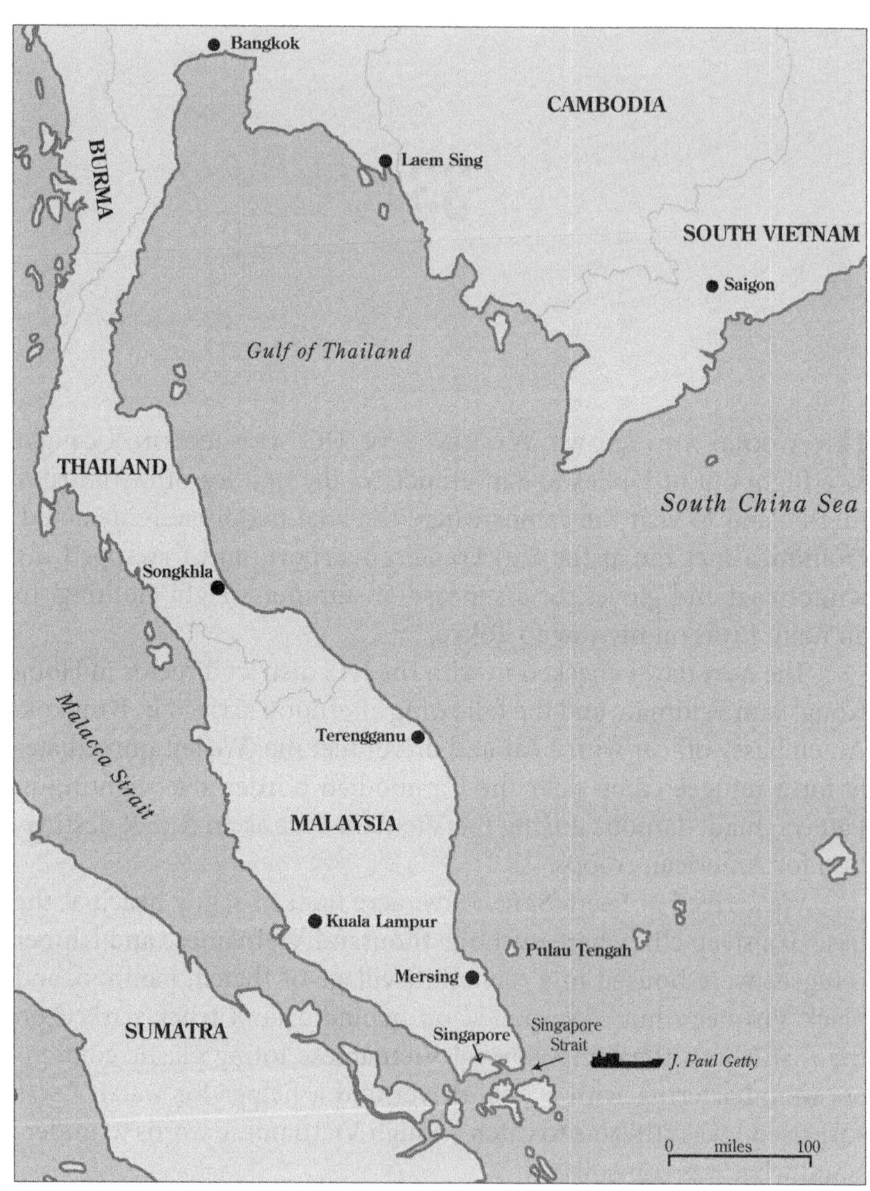

Thailand, Malaysia, and Singapore

"I saw some of the refugees bartering for water up on the road," I said to Mr. Hall.

"Yes," he said. "The only well in the camp is dry, and they have to buy water from the Thais. The UNHCR gives the Thai government money to provide food and water, but delivery is spotty and sometimes inadequate, particularly fresh meat, fish, and vegetables."

"How do the refugees get money?" I asked.

"They've brought every bit of wealth they had with them, of course, dollars, gold, Vietnamese piastres, old US military script, whatever," Hall answered. "In most cases it's not much, but they pool what they have to pay for the things the camp needs."

Laem Sing Camp, Thailand. The camp, no larger than two acres, housed 1,055 boat people, mostly Vietnamese, but including 350 Cambodians and some Chinese.

We picked our way along paths between flimsy bamboo and Visqueen shelters. The only open space I found, and the only level ground, was used for a volleyball court. I was surprised to come upon a more substantial bamboo and thatch structure with a peaked roof and a platform, open to the front, that appeared to be a stage. A large, tinsel Christmas star hung at the peak of the roof, and a tinsel sign said, "Merry Christmas." The interior was adorned with green and red

Christmas decorations. I looked at Hall; it was past Epiphany, when such decorations were traditionally taken down.

The best edifice in Laem Sing camp. Built by the refugees themselves, it served as both a church and a school. Three weeks after Christmas, the decorations remained up. "They're all we have," the refugees told the author.

"They really don't have anything else to decorate the place with," he said with a shrug. "This is the Baptist church. There's a Catholic church, also. They use the buildings as schools, too. Some of the refugees are teachers. They never stop teaching their kids. They have English classes for the adults, too."

Tam Ky all over again, I thought, remembering the roads lined with children on their way to and from school. Despite the rudely constructed dwellings, I found an order about the camp, a sense of activity.

"The camp is run by an elected committee of twenty-three refugees," Hall explained. "There are three language groups here, Viet, Khmer, and Chinese. Each elects its own chief, and of the three, one is elected as overall chief. They have popular suffrage and the secret ballot."

Late in the afternoon, my embassy escort and I returned to Bangkok. The next morning, Saturday, I flew to Songkhla on an embassy aircraft with assistant secretary of state for the Far East and South Asia, Robert Oakley. He was on his way to meet with the vice governor of Songkhla Province. He insisted that I attend a reception planned for him by the vice governor later that afternoon. I was reluctant because I had only packed along a tan, corduroy jacket that was crumpled up in my canvas bag.

US vice consul Robert Hayashida met us in Songkhla and, after taking Ambassador Oakley and me to a hotel, took me on to the refugee camp. Unlike Laem Sing, the camp was at least on level ground, but a similar collection of bamboo, thatch, and black Visqueen shelters housed the over 1,200 refugees. The Swedish UNHCR representative said that due to the vice governor's policy of forcing refugee boats back to sea, the camp population was growing more slowly.

He introduced me to six men, recent arrivals from Rack Gia, Vietnam, who related a tragic story. With their families, they had set sail from Vietnam three weeks earlier, but about twenty miles off the coast, their overcrowded boat broke up in rough seas. They were taken aboard a Thai fishing vessel. The fishermen, however, were afraid if they took the refugees into port they themselves would be arrested for transporting the refugees. They took the Vietnamese to a stretch of uninhabited coast, but because of rough seas, the fishing boat could go no closer than three hundred yards from the shore. The Thais forced the refugees over the side and made them swim for shore. The six men were the only survivors. Their wives and children, fourteen in all, drowned.

Back at the hotel, I pulled my crumpled corduroy jacket out of my canvas bag, but I needn't have worried about the wrinkles; by the time I got to the reception at province headquarters, the folds and creases were gone in the hot, tropical afternoon, steamed from the inside out.

Ambassador Oakley took me in tow, introducing me grandly as the special assistant to the commissioner of the United States Immigration and Naturalization Service, a position that at best I held only unofficially.

At dinner, the ambassador and the vice-governor were effusive in their toasts to each other, overly so, I sensed. I suspected their private meeting earlier in the day had not gone well. My suspicions were confirmed when the vice governor publicly boasted of forcing refugee boats back to sea, seemingly rubbing it in to Oakley.

Three years after the war, the Thais were alarmed by the rapid buildup of Vietnamese refugees on their shores and annoyed at the refusal of western governments, in particular the United States, to take them off their hands. Attacks on refugee boats at sea by fishermen and pirates had become increasingly common, and the United States thought the Thai government was encouraging it.

Oakley had hoped to persuade the vice governor to protect the boat people from such depredations, but several times the vice governor repeated that he would continue to force refugee boats back out to sea, towing them beyond the twelve-mile territorial limit with Thai Navy vessels.

The vice governor taunted Oakley, asking if the United States was prepared to take the refugees off Thailand's hands. Placed on the defensive and his hands tied, Oakley could only respond legalistically, that the boat people were fleeing economic hardship, not political oppression, and therefore most were not eligible for asylum in the United States.

Frustrated, early Sunday morning, Oakley had flown back to Bangkok. After seeing him off, Hayashida returned, and we had breakfast on the lanai. The cloudless blue sky promised another pleasant tropical day. I was scheduled to fly on to Kuala Lumpur at one o'clock.

As we lingered over coffee, a slender, middle-aged European pushed his way through the bushes to the railing of the lanai and interrupted us. Hayashida quickly introduced the man as a French doctor with Médecins Sans Frontièrs.

"The Thai Navy is preparing to tow a refugee boat out to sea," he said. "I counted thirty-four men, women, and children on the boat, mostly children. They've been at sea three days, and their boat drifted in during the night. They have no fresh water, and the children are sick from drinking seawater. They were boarded and robbed by pirates. The men were beaten up. The women have been raped. I did the best I could to treat them on the deck of their boat. I don't think they can survive another night at sea, particularly the children."

"Where are they?" Hayashida asked.

"At the government quay, but you'd better hurry. They're about to get underway."

Hayashida and I threw enough baht on the table to cover our checks and raced to Hayashida's car.

34

THE BRONZE-SKINNED PEOPLE CROUCHING on the packed deck of the wooden fishing boat had fallen back into an eerie silence. Not even the babies cried. Their gaze seemed to focus straight ahead yet fixed on nothing. Out of the corner of my eye, I saw the Thai official start towards us. The crew of the gunboat prepared to cast off the lines.

What must be going through their minds? Nobody in the world wants them, not even my own country. They're about to be taken out on the ocean and dumped like garbage. WHERE ARE YOU, GOD? What do you expect of me?

The answer came with a clarity that startled me. Every bit of me, every lesson learned from my parents, my church, and my training, seemed to come together. I turned to Hayashida. "Tell the aide that if the vice governor will let the Vietnamese go into the refugee camp, I will guarantee they will be taken to the United States."

"Do you have that authority?" Hayashida looked at me incredulously.

"Yes," I lied, looking him square in the eye.

I sensed that Hayashida knew I was lying, but he realized at once that it was our only hope. He did as I asked, and the Thai official said he would delay the boat's departure long enough for us to go to the province headquarters and contact the vice governor by radio. I told Hayashida to go. In the meantime, I stood on the dock at the side of the fishing boat, my foot resting on the gunwale, ready to jump onto the crowded deck if my offer was refused and the gunboat got underway with the refugees in tow.

I was breaking US law and was almost certain to lose my job, I could be prosecuted, but I felt at peace with myself, as if I had prepared my entire life for this moment. I was doing the right thing, doing what my conscience required of me, and what, I had decided, my country expected of me. I could work as a clerk in a neighborhood Ace Hardware Store, I thought; my family and I would be all right with that. The refugees would live.

Everything rested with the vice governor believing me and accepting a commitment that I had no authority to make. The Immigration and Nationality Act permitted the attorney general under emergency circumstances to waive other provisions of the act and parole an alien into the United States. It had been done in many circumstances for refugees fleeing Communist regimes in Eastern Europe and Cuba, but such relief was granted to the Vietnamese boat refugees only if they could establish that they had a close association with the United States through a near family relationship or meaningful employment by the United States during the war.

The people on the fishing boat were none of these. They were fishermen from a small island and had had little or no contact with Americans. Even if I could get word to my bosses in Washington, there was little likelihood the far-away bureaucrats would reverse US policy.

Children peer out from the cabin of the refugee boat at Songkhla, Thailand.

If the Thai government accepted my commitment and the refugees were allowed to enter the UNHCR camp, I knew I'd have to convince both the State Department and the Justice Department to honor my commitment to take them on to the United States. I was prepared to wage that battle once I got back to Washington, DC, even if I had to do so as an ex-federal employee.

If I failed, the Thais would repatriate the Vietnamese to their now Communist homeland. Just the previous week, the Thais had signed an agreement with the Socialist Republic of Vietnam permitting the repatriation of the Vietnamese boat people directly to the Communist nation. As unwelcome a result as that would be, at least they'd be alive, I thought.

As I waited for Hayashida to return, I watched the gunboat for any sign of getting underway. Would the sailors physically block me from leaping aboard the fishing boat? Would they forcibly remove me if I did? Or would they tow me out to sea, too?

Hayashida rushed onto the dock with good news. The vice governor would let the refugees land if I put my commitment to take them on to the United States in writing. Relieved, I was only too happy to do so.

Balancing a yellow legal pad on top of a bollard next to the fishing boat, I began to write. I paused over how to sign the letter. In truth, I was a mid-level federal employee, an immigration examiner from San Francisco on temporary detail in Washington, DC. To be credible, I would need cachet. Keying on Ambassador Oakley's introduction of me at the vice governor's reception the previous afternoon as the INS commissioner's assistant, I signed myself "Special Assistant to the Commissioner."

Hayashida left for his office to type the letter on State Department letterhead, leaving me at my post beside the fishing boat. When he returned, I signed it, and he presented it to the vice governor's aide.

Promptly, the Thai sailors cast off their tether to the sampan, and the gunboat departed.

"Are you able to move your boat over to the refugee camp?" I asked the refugee captain, gesturing to the colony of thatch and Visqueen huts visible about five hundred yards away. To my surprise, the captain looked alarmed. Several of the boat committee gathered around him.

"We want to go to Australia," he said.

Dumbfounded, I called Hayashida's interpreter over and explained again that they were being given haven in the refugee camp.

"We want to go to Australia," the captain repeated.

"What are you going to do for food?" I argued, growing exasperated. "Your children are sick. You have no money to buy food or fuel. You can't even keep your motor running."

"The Thai official told us if we went into the camp, they would send us back to Vietnam," the captain responded. "We prefer to take our chances at sea."

The refugees had less than a day's ration of rice, no fresh water, and an unreliable engine. They knew their chances of survival at sea were slim to none, yet they wanted to press on rather than risk being returned to their now Communist homeland.

The refugees wanted to get to Australia, but their map, a page torn from a schoolbook, did not even show the continent. Their compass had been recovered from the instrument panel of a downed aircraft.

"No, they won't," I argued emphatically. "I know about their agreement with the Communists, but I've signed a letter guaranteeing the Thai government that you will be taken to the United States. You will be in the camp only long enough for Vice Consul Hayashida and me to make the arrangements. You will not be sent back to Vietnam."

I had the interpreter read a copy of the letter I had signed and Hayashida had given to the vice governor's aide:

> "Pursuant to the authority delegated to me by the Attorney General of the United States of America and under the provisions of Section 212(d)(5) of the Immigration and Nationality Act as Amended, I am authorizing the parole into the United States of the thirty-four (34) below named citizens of the Socialist Republic of Vietnam currently detained by the Royal Thai Navy in Songkhla."

The body of the letter contained each of their names, dates, and places of birth, which I had the interpreter read, too.

"You will be in the camp only long enough for me to make the arrangements to take you on to the United States," I promised again. "The US government will not abandon you." Having turned its back on these people's country just three years earlier, I knew that was an awful stretch. The refugees continued to look at me dubiously. I showed them my official passport and my INS credentials, letting them pass them among themselves.

"I spent two years in your country fighting the Communists," I pleaded. "I was in Tam Ky, far away from my own family. Millions of Americans were in your country fighting the Communists. Those of us who were there with you will not forget you now."

Finally, their leaders nodded their heads; yes, they would go to the camp, the leader said. But yet another issue arose.

"We need food," the captain said. "The Thais told us we have to buy our own food in the camp, and we have only twenty dollars. Some of our people are naked. We don't want the people already in the camp to see us that way."

Finally, something I can be sure is going to work, I thought. I gave my newly acquired American Express green card to Hayashida's assistant who rushed off to a nearby market.

The fishing boat managed the few hundred yards to the camp and beached just as Hayashida's assistant arrived with two hundred kilos of rice, two crates of live chickens, cooking oil, and two boxes of T-shirts, women's blouses, and pants he had purchased at a nearby market.

A large and curious welcoming committee met the new arrivals, and after donning the clothing Hayashida's assistant had brought, the refugees scurried ashore. Their first order of business was to seek word about the fate of the other boats and families that had fled Phuc Quoc Island with them, but no one in the camp had heard of them.

After taking a few pictures, I felt confident leaving the refugees in the hands of Vice Consul Hayashida and the UNHCR representative. They were safe for now. The failure of the US to accept the Vietnamese as refugees was one thing, but it would be career-ending for a bureaucrat in either the State Department or the Justice Department to hand them back to Thailand where they were likely to be deported to Communist Vietnam.

The men and boys from the refugee boat in the UNHCR camp newly attired in clothing the author purchased for them in a local market. They did not want photos to be taken of the women and girls.

It was best the Thais not know I had lied to them. I had not told Hayashida, feeling it safest for the refugees that I just keep my mouth shut. I knew I had a lot to explain when I got back to Washington, DC, in a week before their future, or mine, would be set. In the meantime, I had a job to finish.

Hayashida drove me back to the hotel to retrieve my bag and then on to the airport. I caught my scheduled flight to Kuala Lumpur as if nothing had happened. The whole event had transpired in less than an hour.

35

I WAS MET IN KUALA LUMPUR, BY A YOUNG CONSULAR OFFICER, Joe Getier, who took me to my hotel. The next day utilizing a car and driver furnished by the embassy, we drove back across the Malay Peninsula to Trenganu, a port city on the South China Sea and the site of a large refugee camp. The next morning at breakfast, we met a team of three INS officers who were destined to the camp to interview refugees who had been identified as potentially eligible under the US criteria to be resettled in the United States.

When we arrived at the camp, we learned of another tragedy. The UNHCR representative told us that the week before, the Malaysian Navy intercepted a refugee boat with twenty-one men, women, and children as they approached Trenganu. The Vietnamese were refused permission to land, and the boat anchored off the mouth of a nearby river. During the night, a storm came up. The boat broke free from its mooring anchor and capsized. In an outcome duplicating a similar tragedy I had learned of in Thailand, only the stronger men were able to swim to shore. Fifteen women and children drowned.

I watched as the immigration officers interviewed refugees, and then I participated in a couple myself. Each of the hopeful applicants had been pre-identified by the UNHCR and then screened by a State Department officer for their degree of association with the United States. One claimed to have an uncle in the United States, status unknown, another a cousin, neither relationship close enough to qualify the refugee as the immediate relative of a US citizen. A third applicant, upon questioning, admitted that his claimed position with the

US government was as a laborer, working for a US contractor, also not qualifying. The criteria required that he had held a "supervisory or otherwise meaningful position" in the US government for at least one year subsequent to January 1, 1962.

I broke away and toured the camp with the UNHCR representative and then talked to a Malaysian official. Over two thousand Vietnamese lived in the Visqueen and bamboo huts. Many had been there over a year, some since the fall of Saigon three years earlier. Seven of the refugees were doctors and were able to care for the camp population with medicine and supplies furnished by the Malaysian Red Crescent Society.

A child in Mersing Camp, Malaysia, who drew a ship with an American flag for the author as a way of communicating his family's hopes.

The next day, Getier and I continued down the coast to Mersing, the site of another refugee camp. We stayed in a government guesthouse fronted by a pristine, white-sand beach and the turquoise sea. The three-story, white-stucco building was bordered by royal fan palms. Wooden shutters hung at the sides of the unglazed windows, and we slept under mosquito netting.

The Malaysian camps, we found, had been allocated more space, and were less crowded. They were also better provisioned as the UNHCR channeled money for food through the Red Crescent Society. Besides rice, the refugees received fish every week and meat every other week.

The camp at Palau Tengah had recently been relocated to a deserted island, and we traveled out to it by launch. Malaysian officials said that eventually all the Vietnamese would be moved to unpopulated, offshore islands to better isolate their rapidly expanding numbers from the local Malaysian population.

The boat people relocated to Pulau Tengah island by the Malaysian government await the author as his launch approaches the shore.

Tired, sweaty, caked by road dust, late that afternoon, we drove across the causeway to Singapore and pulled up in front of the low, white Raffles Hotel. After we finished registering, we edged into the dark-paneled bar just off the lobby, the watering hole frequented by Rudyard Kipling and Somerset Maugham. We ordered Singapore Slings from a white-jacketed Chinese waiter. That evening after I cleaned up and put on a jacket and tie, I went back downstairs to the Elizabethan Grill Room and enjoyed Consommé Kipling and Paupiette de Rouget Maugham.

John Norris, the third secretary, met me when I checked in at the embassy the next morning, Friday.

"We've been waiting for you," Norris said. "We've got a problem, and your office says you can help. An American-owned supertanker, the *J. Paul Getty*, has been anchored out in the roadstead for the past two days. It picked up a boatload of Vietnamese refugees at sea, but the Singapore government will not let the *Getty* land them here in Singapore. Nor will it permit it to transit the straits with the refugees on board. It's costing Getty Oil one thousand dollars every hour its tanker is idle. Ambassador Holdridge asks if you'll go right out."

The relayed instruction, "Mr. Harpold will take care of it," was puzzlingly vague. I was certain that by then the INS district director in Hong Kong, Sam Feldman, knew about my unauthorized parole of the thirty-four refugees in Songkhla. Or maybe he didn't. I had not checked in with him since I had left Hong Kong, and maybe he had not heard through State Department channels. But what could I do with the boat people picked up by the *Getty*, other than what I had done in Songkhla, parole them all? I decided calling Feldman could result only in narrowing my options once I was aboard the supertanker.

The *Getty* was anchored about thirty miles out in the roadstead, and Norris and I were soon on our way out to it in a launch. On the way, I learned more about the Singaporean policy.

"It's not just about the boat people," Norris explained. "Singapore simply does not want immigrants, and they're afraid they'll be stuck with the Vietnamese if the United States doesn't resettle them. They tow refugee boats that make it to Singapore back out to sea, and as happened to the *Getty*, they don't permit any vessel that picks them up to land them in Singapore. We know of at least five cases where refugees, including children, are permanent guests on the boats of the Singaporean fishermen who rescued them.

"In the case of the *Getty*," Norris continued, "they not only refuse to let the Vietnamese ashore; they won't let the vessel transit the Singapore Straits with refugees aboard."

The ramifications of Singapore's policy were far-reaching. If vessels like the *Getty* that stopped and rescued distressed boat people were refused passage through the Singapore Straits, one of the busiest commercial waterways in the world, they would no longer stop for Vietnamese boats in trouble or adrift. More boat people would die at sea. Like Thailand and Malaysia, Singapore was not going to provide temporary haven for the refugees unless the United States and other free-world countries took the Vietnamese off their hands.

Based on what I had already found in the camps, it was not likely the refugees aboard the *Getty* would be eligible for resettlement under the narrow US policy either. Typically, they would be peasant farmers or fishermen.

I understood that a change in US policy would not happen overnight; at best, my report would trigger the start of things. Under present law, it would be up to the attorney general and the secretary of state to decide whether the boat people were legitimate exceptions to US policy and that I was acting out of humanitarian necessity in paroling the refugees on board the small boat in Songkhla and now those of the *J. Paul Getty*. If not, not even Commissioner Castillo could save my job.

The *Getty*, en route to the Persian Gulf to pick up a cargo of crude oil, was riding high out of the water, and we climbed up the hull on a Jacob's ladder, not an unfamiliar experience for an immigration officer. The refugees' small boat, gaily painted red and blue, had been hoisted onto the deck. The crew was Italian, but as we were escorted along the steel-walled passageways to the ship's lounge, I heard sounds I had never heard before on a merchant ship: the squeals and joyous laughter of little children racing up and down the corridors. It was impossible not to smile, and I noticed that the crewmen did, too, often scooping up a small child and evoking more squeals as they lifted the youngster over their heads. Captain Salefi, a slight, middle-aged man with a receding hairline, met us in the lounge.

"Never has a ship been so happy as we are with these children on board," the captain said. The refugees had been trying to reach the Philippines, he said, but still had more than 450 miles to go when they were rescued.

"They crossed our bow several times, waving their shirts and clothing," Captain Salefi related. "We stopped and allowed them to come alongside. I sent my first mate down to examine their boat. It was leaking badly; water was mixing with the fuel and oil, fouling the engine. At that point, I had a moral and legal obligation to bring them aboard the *J. Paul Getty*."

With the help of an interpreter, I interviewed the captain of the Vietnamese boat, Vo Dick Thanh, and his cousin, Vo No. Vo No had been employed by the US defense attaché's office at the end of the war and been offered the chance to be evacuated with the Americans when Saigon fell in 1975.

"I didn't go," Vo No explained. "There was so much confusion, and I couldn't find my wife and four little children. I wouldn't go without them. When I found them, the Communists made us move to a New Economic Area near Nha Trang, and my wife and I were forced to work clearing the jungle. My cousin, Thanh, and I managed to keep in touch and plan our escape."

"I had a fishing boat in Nha Trang," Thanh said, taking up the story from his cousin. "I had a fifty-five-gallon drum on the boat. The Communists gave me two liters of diesel fuel for each fishing trip, but I used only one and a half liters and saved the rest in the drum. I also took one rock each trip until I had enough ballast to risk a voyage on the sea. We collected fresh water in plastic bottles and hid them beneath the surface of the water near shore."

In the meantime, Vo No worked to secure the goodwill of the Communist camp commander by giving him the fish he had caught in his spare time. Eventually, he started to get passes to go into town. When Thanh finally communicated that his boat was ready, Vo No convinced the camp commander to allow him and his family to go into town on a Sunday afternoon to view a movie they were interested in seeing. But instead of going to see the movie, he and his family walked to Nha Trang, forty kilometers away.

That night, they set sail on Thanh's fishing boat. They had planned that only their families, twelve people, would go, but fifteen others who knew of the plot simply came along. They included a policeman, a civil servant, and their families.

"We had a map that showed only Vietnam and a hand compass used by soldiers," Thanh said. "I set a course of 90 degrees, due east. We wanted to go to any country out of Vietnam."

"That course would have brought them to the Philippines," Captain Salefi confirmed. "But they would have had to pass through a shoal area labeled on the charts as the North Shoal Area. Without charts and navigation aids, they would have destroyed their boat. As it was, they were almost out of food. We found only three bags of rice on board."

"We really didn't need that much rice anyway," Vo No said. "We were mostly too seasick to eat."

The twenty-seven Vietnamese rescued by the Getty pose in front of their boat, which had been lifted to the deck of the supertanker.

With Norris helping, I interviewed the refugees and gathered their personal data. Other than Vo No, nine of the ten men on board were fishermen. Despite his employment with the defense attaché's office and the offer to evacuate him with the Americans, his position was not significant enough to qualify under the criteria in place after the war. It didn't matter. I had decided to parole everyone. No one would be left on the *J. Paul Getty*.

Captain Salefi insisted we stay and have lunch with him and the crew, but the meal turned out to be not a mere meal but at least an eight-course Italian feast, complete at the end with a bowl of spumoni and expresso. As we pushed back our chairs, the chef, a large man, wearing a towering, white chef's hat and an apron, appeared in the doorway. A broad grin separated his heavy jowls. On each arm, he carried a delighted Vietnamese child.

The American-owned supertanker, the J. Paul Getty, at anchor at a roadstead forty miles east of Singapore. The Singapore government refused to let it transit the Singapore Straits with refugees onboard and refused to take in the refugees themselves.

"He lets the children help him cook," Captain Salefi explained.

It was dark when Norris and I returned to the American embassy. I prepared a letter similar to the one I had penned in Songkhla, guaranteeing the government of Singapore that the twenty-seven refugees on the *Getty* would be taken to the United States for resettlement. The ambassador had waited in his office and, after penning a transmittal letter, had it delivered immediately to the Singaporean government. By ten p.m., the refugees were taken off the *Getty* to be housed in a refugee camp, and the supertanker was underway through the Singapore Straits to the Persian Gulf.

Saturday morning, I flew from Singapore back to Bangkok where I met with International Rescue Committee director, Nan Borton, and others who worked for voluntary refugee resettlement agencies, volags. They heard that I had paroled the boatload of refugees in Songkhla, but believing I had the authority to do so were taken with the possibility of an overall loosening of the strict US refugee policy, not only for boat refugees but also for the Hmong and lowland Lao. An estimated eighty thousand of them, US allies during the war and now fleeing the Communist regime in Laos, had built up in refugee camps in northern Thailand along the Laotian border.

The volags worked closely with the embassy, and I was encouraged that, though they knew I had paroled the refugees in Songkhla, they did not know I had misrepresented my authority. I was pretty sure the embassy and Feldman in Hong Kong knew, but I was confident there would be enough bureaucratic churn over it to give me time to get to Castillo. I was scheduled to fly back to Washington, DC, the next day. I kept up the charade with the volags, some of whom were Thai nationals.

I told the volags that given the congressional hearing scheduled for Wednesday, there simply wasn't enough time on my trip to visit one of the land camps, but the land refugees would not be forgotten. Ms. Borton was soon to return to Washington, DC, and I promised her a meeting with Commissioner Castillo.

Later that day, I flew on to Hong Kong. Since I was arriving late in the evening, I insisted that INS district director, Sam Feldman, not meet me but promised that we would get together for breakfast Sunday morning instead. At the airport, my bags did not arrive with me on my flight, including a cardboard box of artifacts I had gathered in the camps and wanted to display at the congressional hearing now just four days away. After a half-hour spent convincing Cathay Pacific Airlines of the importance of finding my bags, I walked out of the now-deserted terminal to the curb where I expected to find a cab, but only a lone, black Mercedes limo waited. A Chinese man wearing a chauffer's uniform approached me.

"Are you Mr. Harpold? he asked.

Damn you, Sam, I thought. I had met him for the first time on my way to Thailand and found him oddly solicitous, insisting on turning over his private office to me while I waited for my connecting flight to Bangkok.

The chauffer drove from the airport through the traffic tunnel under Victoria Bay and pulled up at the foot of the broad steps that led up to the chandeliered lobby of the Hong Kong Hilton. I was met at the curb by the assistant manager and escorted past the front desk to a tenth-floor room overlooking city hall and the bay. A basket of fruit and a pink cake lettered "Welcome Mr. Harpold" awaited me along with a fully stocked bar. I couldn't know at that point if the Hilton had comped Sam the room or if for some personal reason he had paid for it himself, but I was too tired to sample any of it except the bed.

Feldman arrived at 10 a.m., and we ordered a room service breakfast. I probed for reactions to the commitments I had made to the refugees in Songkhla and on the *J. Paul Getty*. Feldman was responsible for INS operations in Southeast Asia, including processing and transporting the refugees I had paroled to the United States—if my promises to them were to be honored.

"I imagine that'll be worked out when you get back to Washington," Feldman said enigmatically.

"Okay, Sam, what's up?" I asked.

"My tour here is up in a few months, but I haven't decided where I want to go next," he said earnestly.

"I don't have anything to do with assignments, Sam," I interjected, seeing where this was going.

"You're friends with Mr. Castillo," Feldman said knowingly. "Sometimes things come up informally or in conversation, and when it does, I want to go to Boston, Honolulu, or San Francisco."

"I'll tell you what, Sam," I said. "There are sixty-one refugees waiting in those camps that I have made commitments to. Whether they'll be brought to the US will be up to someone higher than you, me, or Commissioner Castillo. I may spend the rest of my life fighting to get them to the US, but when they're ready to come, I don't want any glitches, no lost files or missing fingerprint checks. When they arrive in the US, I'll be telling Mr. Castillo what a fine job you do out here."

"I'll let you know which position I want when I get closer to my transfer date," Feldman called after me as I stepped onto the jet way at the Pan Am departure gate that noon. As a parting gesture, he arranged with the Pan Am station manager for a vacant seat beside me on the otherwise full flight across the Pacific. My lap and the adjoining seat covered with papers and documents, I worked through the night on my report.

When I arrived at San Francisco International Airport in the morning, Dominica was waiting with my winter coat. After a hug and a kiss, I was off on the last leg of my journey, to Washington, DC. I was too tired to worry much about what would happen upon my arrival.

36

"OH, GOOD!" MRS. HART EXCLAIMED in her soft southern voice as I pushed through the double glass doors of the commissioner's office on Monday morning. "Mr. Castillo wants to see you right away." The door to the inner office was closed, indicating he was already in a meeting. "It'll be just a few minutes. Mr. Noto and Mr. Wack are in there now," she said, a note of caution in her voice.

It had been eight days since I had penned the letter to the Thai government on the dock in Songkhla committing the United States to take the thirty-four Vietnamese refugees about to be towed out to sea and abandoned; three days since I had made a similar unauthorized commitment to take in twenty-seven refugees rescued by the *J. Paul Getty*. I wondered what had transpired since then, what had been the reaction here in the headquarters of the INS. Feldman must have known something; why had he been so close-mouthed?

The door to the inner office opened, and two somber, grey-headed men in dark suits emerged: deputy commissioner Mario Noto and associate commissioner for examinations, Karl Wack, the number two and three men in the agency. Neither man greeted me. Each shot me a dark look as he passed.

"You can go in now," Mrs. Hart said, and I took courage in the confident tone of her voice. She had seen many commissioners come and go, and her demeanor signaled to people she liked what to expect as they passed into the commissioner's inner office. I took a seat on the couch at the side of Commissioner Castillo's desk.

"Those guys want me to fire you," Castillo said, his face breaking into its characteristic grin.

"Commissioner, they were going to tow that boat out to sea and cut it adrift. The people would have died," I protested. "They were mostly women and children."

Castillo turned serious and handed me a newspaper clipping with a note attached. "Have you seen this?" he asked.

The article had been clipped from the *New York Times*, and the headline read, "Thai Irritation on Refugees Grows."[1] It was written by Henry Kamm, the Bangkok bureau chief of the *Times* and described the plight of the boat people and the diplomatic efforts, including Ambassador Oakley's visit to Songkhla, to persuade the Thais to stop forcing the small boats overcrowded with Vietnamese refugees back to sea. The final paragraphs were about the refugee boat in Songkhla.

> A boat carrying 34 refugees sought time to repair its engine but was ordered by local authorities at gun point to leave for the open sea within ten minutes.
>
> The action was averted by the presence here of Michael Harpold, special assistant to the director of the United States Immigration and Naturalization Service. On his own authority he guaranteed that the United States would accept the refugees, and they were allowed ashore.

"Commissioner, I could never have walked away and lived with myself. I apologize for usurping the title," I pleaded. I was surprised to see the incident had been picked up in the news.

"Read the note," Castillo urged.

"Leonel—You are to be congratulated on having staff that can take the initiative and act to save refugees' lives when they are in such peril." It was signed by Wells Klein, a prominent New York philanthropist, who since World War II had dedicated his life and resources to helping Eastern European refugees.

No more was said about firing me.

1. January 23, 1978.

On Wednesday, the day before the Congressional hearing, Mr. Castillo told me Attorney General Bell and Secretary of State Vance had concurred in my parole of the refugees.

The next morning, the dais was full when chairman Joshua Eilberg gaveled the House Subcommittee on Immigration, Citizenship, and International Law to order. After introductory remarks, he called on Commissioner Castillo. Soon into his testimony, Castillo described my use of the attorney general's parole authority to save Vietnamese refugees at the dock at Songkhla.

"I have assured Mr. Harpold that we will back him in his parole commitment and that arrangements will be made for these refugees to come to the United States," Castillo said. "For humanitarian reasons and our nation's own special responsibility to Indochinese boat-case refugees, it is the attorney general's present judgment that the situation of the boat-case refugees is an emergent one and our favorable response under the circumstances is in the public interest and warranted," Commissioner Castillo continued.

Chairman Eilberg looked concerned, as did several other committee members. The executive branch's use of the attorney general's parole authority for Indochina refugees, instead of asking Congress for legislation, was a sore point with the subcommittee. The authority contained in the Immigration and Nationality Act was meant to provide an avenue for relief of an individual in distress, conservative members of Congress said, not for broad-scale application in international situations. The chairman was not ready to let go of the issue.

"Commissioner, this is sort of a technical question," Chairman Eilberg said when Castillo paused for questions. "As you stated, a member of the INS on the spot promised to parole a group of refugees on January 14. For the record, would you please state what authority this individual has to make this commitment?"

I bit my lip.

Castillo winged it. "All our officers abroad have authority to exercise discretion in what they feel are emergency cases. They act in my name, and my authority is, in turn, delegated from the attorney general," Castillo said, accepting responsibility but ducking the broader issue of the attorney general's authority.

Chairman Eilberg paused. His gaze turned from Commissioner Castillo to me and then back. After a moment, he moved on. Undoubtedly aware of the *New York Times* mention of the incident, he let the matter drop.

Castillo went on to relate details of what I had found on my trip: the self-organization of the camps, the cleanliness of the refugees despite their primitive shelters, the building of schools and churches, and lessons taught to the children on the decks of boats even while at sea. The refugees were for the most part self-employed fishermen and farmers who fled their homeland because the Communists confiscated their catches and crops, Castillo said.

Castillo passed some of the artifacts I had brought back with me to the subcommittee members: a GI hand compass used by one of the boats to navigate at sea; the map of Southeast Asia torn from a schoolbook used by the refugee boat I had encountered in Songkhla. Expressing awe of the families braving the open sea with such rudimentary navigation tools, the congressmen and congresswomen examined the items reverently passing them from hand to hand along the dais.

It struck me that just three years earlier, these same members of Congress had voted to end all economic and military aid to South Vietnam, crippling their economy and the government and paving the way for the full-scale invasion across its borders by the Communist North. But I was too full of hope for the boat refugees' future to dwell long on whether they were thinking about that now.

By Friday afternoon, regulations had been drawn up within the Department of Justice specifically delegating the authority of the attorney general to immigration officers to parole "boat refugees without offers of resettlement from other countries whose admission is considered necessary from a humanitarian standpoint." In cases similar to that faced by the *J. Paul Getty*, immigration officers were empowered to give letters to foreign governments confirming parole status for those picked up at sea by US flag or US owned vessels.

I was elated.

Later, Commissioner Castillo gave a copy of my report to nationally syndicated columnist Jack Anderson. Headlining the story, "Asian Refugees Fate Hinges on U.S.," Anderson devoted his full column to my trip.[2] In the final paragraph, he quoted from my report's final paragraph:

> "We should adopt and announce as policy," [Harpold] urged, "our willingness to accept and resettle refugees rescued by vessels at sea and those who arrive by boat on the shores of those countries bordering the South China Sea. Only by doing so can we ensure that masters of commercial vessels and the governments of Malaysia, Thailand and Singapore will treat the boat people humanely."

In Prairie du Sac, Wisconsin, my mother read the column in the *Wisconsin State Journal* and wrote me a letter I would forever cherish. "You have certainly had some experiences for a small-town, country boy! I hope this contact with the hard side of life doesn't leave you calloused to it all, and evidently it hasn't." She then paraphrased Portia from Shakespeare's *The Merchant of Venice*:

> "The quality of mercy is not strained. It blesses him that gives and him who takes."

The CBS *60 Minutes* crew went to Thailand, and correspondent Ed Bradley was filmed pulling an elderly woman from the surf as the crowded fishing boat she had arrived on beached and overturned. Other TV networks quickly followed, filming their own, on-the-scene stories. A steady parade of senators, representatives, and administration officials traveled to Southeast Asia to see for themselves.

Commissioner Castillo went, too, following the same trail to refugee camps as I had. After he returned, in speaking engagements across the country, he reminded audiences of America's moral obligation to provide a haven for the boat people. In presentations to community groups and high school and college students in the area, he toted along the model refugee boat carved in the camp at Palau Tengah that I had brought back with me.

---

2. *Washington Post*, March 15, 1978.

Spurred by growing public calls for action, Congress began work in earnest on an all-encompassing refugee law, one that would include the UN definition of the term:

> A person who is outside his country of birth and fears to return because of a well-founded fear of persecution for reasons of race, religion, nationality, political opinion or membership in a particular social group.

Until new law was enacted, the Carter administration told Congress it would increase the number of paroles for Indochina refugees to 50,000 annually, including 12,500 for the remainder of 1978. In fact, over the next three years, 242,000 Vietnamese, Laotian, and Cambodian refugees were brought to the United States for resettlement.

On April 12, 1978, Patricia M. Derian, assistant secretary of state for Human Rights and Humanitarian Affairs, Ambassador Robert Oakley at her side, testified before the House Subcommittee on Immigration, Citizenship, and International Law:

> We strongly believe, Mr. Chairman, that they [the boat people] are political refugees. There is a clear and consistent pattern of violation of human rights in these countries, as the new communist governments restructure their societies. Many of the refugees have suffered economic hardship as well, but this is a result of economic discrimination for political ends—often to the extreme of refusing former members of the middle class the means to earn a livelihood.
>
> The risks undertaken by such refugees, both to themselves and to their loved ones, paint a picture of individuals being driven by motivation far stronger than economic advantage. It is almost certain that many perish at sea. Most refugees indicate they fully appreciated this danger when they fled. In any case, those who escape would clearly face severe retribution if they were returned to Vietnam.

With so many public figures and the media traveling to Southeast Asia to see first-hand the plight of the boat people, I soon found myself relegated to the sidelines. But after being smothered by our disappointment in Vietnam, America's heart had begun to open up again. Calls to give the boat people haven in the United States met with little dissent. Americans stepped forward to sponsor the Vietnamese, help them get jobs, enroll their kids in school, and introduce them at church.

Late in May, the refugees I had rescued at the dock in Thailand and those rescued by the *J. Paul Getty* arrived in the United States to begin their new lives.

In September, in a single line in the appropriation enacted that year for the Departments of State, Justice, Commerce and the Judiciary, Congress authorized the Treasury to pay me $242, reimbursement for the food and clothing I had purchased for the refugees I had rescued that Sunday morning in Songkhla, Thailand.

By then, I was back at my desk in San Francisco, routinely considering petitions for family members and temporary workers and interviewing applicants for immigrant status.

I had done my bit.

EPILOGUE

Dimond Courthouse, Juneau, Alaska, March 27, 1997

"What are some of the freedoms protected by the Bill of Rights?" I asked the prim, grey-haired Vietnamese lady seated in front of my desk, an applicant for naturalization. She was seventy years old and worked as a laundress at the Alaska Laundry just across the street from my hotel in downtown Juneau.

"Sir, the Bill of Rights of the United States Constitution. The First Amendment," she began.

From habit, I reached for an ink eraser and began scrubbing the edges of the two small color photos she had submitted, one to be glued onto her Naturalization Certificate if she passed, the other for her file. I would ask her to sign her name on the roughened area when she completed the American history and government test, which I administered orally.

She continued, "Congress shall make no law respecting an establishment of religion, or prohibiting the free exercise thereof; or abridging the freedom of speech, or of the press, or the right of the people peaceably to assemble, and to petition the government for a redress of grievances.

"The Second Amendment," she intoned. "A well-regulated militia, being necessary to the security of a free state, the right of the people to keep and bear arms, shall not be infringed.

"The Third Amendment. No soldier shall, in time of peace, be quartered in any house without the consent of the owner, nor in time of war, but in a manner prescribed by law."

Astonished, I stopped what I was doing and listened.

"The Fourth Amendment. The right of the people to be secure in their persons, houses, papers, and effects, against unreasonable searches and seizures, shall not be violated, and no warrants shall issue, but upon probable cause, supported by oath or affirmation, and particularly describing the place to be searched, and the persons or things to be seized.

"The Fifth Amendment. . . ."

In over fifteen years of examining applicants for naturalization since leaving Washington, DC, I had never met anyone who had memorized the entire Bill of Rights. Seeking to elicit a basic understanding of freedom of speech, religion, assembly, and the press, precepts Asians had not been steeped in from birth, I asked questions about the Bill of Rights. But citizenship classes for most immigrants in Southeast Alaska were ad hoc if available at all. Most petitioners for naturalization struggled to identify even two or three of the freedoms enumerated in the First Amendment.

For a moment, my mind traveled back to Songkhla, Thailand, and the peril-filled voyages of the boat people. Mrs. Nguyen had been one of the strong and the lucky and found refuge in the United States. Her performance on her citizenship test demonstrated why. She and her family had been resettled in Juneau where she raised and educated her children, supporting her family by working in the laundry.

I wanted to hug her, but that was a taboo. Instead, I rose awkwardly to my feet, which at first she interpreted as a sign she should leave.

"No, no, Mrs. Nguyen, stay seated," I cautioned. "You passed. I'm standing because I want to honor you. You've done so well. Tomorrow, you're going to take the Oath of Allegiance and become a US citizen. Congratulations!"

The seemingly frail little woman covered her eyes with her hands, quietly shedding tears. When she looked up, it was with a hopeful grin, as if she had maybe misunderstood and wanted to be told once again.

"You've passed, Mrs. Nguyen," I repeated. "You've done wonderfully well. You're going to be a good citizen."

* * *

The exodus of the boat people continued into the 1990s, but in the months following my trip to the refugee camps, as more Americans learned of the refugees' plight, the public no longer remained indifferent. The country, which had been left exhausted by a long, controversial war with an unsatisfactory ending, had nevertheless once again opened its heart and stepped forward to help. Voluntary refugee resettlement agencies reaped a windfall of sponsors and donations.

In July 1979, a year and a half after my tour of the refugee camps in Southeast Asia, the United Nations High Commissioner for Refugees convened a conference in Geneva, Switzerland, to deal with the still-growing numbers of boat people fleeing the Socialist Republic of Vietnam. Vice president Walter Mondale led the US delegation.

In Geneva, the free-world countries, led by the United States, agreed to accelerate acceptance and resettlement of the refugees. Southeast Asian countries agreed to provide temporary asylum. Vietnam agreed to allow its citizens, identified as eligible in advance, such as those having close relatives in the West, to depart by air to Bangkok where they could be processed by receiving countries.

Within months, Congress passed the Refugee Act of 1980, establishing a base annual quota of fifty thousand and a procedure to obtain authorization for greater numbers to cover emergencies. On March 17, 1980, St. Patrick's Day, President Carter signed it into law. In the decade following, the United States resettled 531,000 Vietnamese boat people and 200,000, Cambodian, Lao, and Hmong "land people." Over time, 1,500,000 boat people were resettled in the West.

One hundred sixty-five thousand South Vietnamese are thought to have died in the Communist regime's re-education camps after the war. Nobody knows for sure how many Vietnamese attempting to flee the country lost their lives on the Gulf of Thailand and the South China Sea. The UNHCR estimates the number who perished at 200,000 to 400,000. Others say a half million.

The End

ACKNOWLEDGMENTS

My daughters, Dominica Doud, Michelle Denning, and Kathryn Harpold, and their mother, Dominica Sylvester, who stood by me and supported me through my frequent travels and long periods away from home, deserve more than I can possibly say. I haven't forgotten. Thank you for your support then and now and for reading the manuscript and offering corrections and encouragement.

My friend and neighbor, Ketchikan artist Dave Rubin, once again created an awesome and memorable cover.

My wife, Elaine, and Norm Dupre of the Local Paper converted my 35 mm half-frame slides from Vietnam into a usable format. Artist and friend Terry Pyles drew the maps and improved the fifty-year-old and often out-of-focus photos.

Sheryn Hara, and her crew at Book Publishers Network, as they did with my historical novel, Jumping the Line, have again produced a book I am proud to present as my own. Editor Julie Scandora set a high standard for it and tolerated no deviation by the author. Melissa Vail Coffman and her husband, Scott Book, did the page and layout design. Laura Zugzda designed the title and laid out the cover.

My writing group fellow members Biz Robbins, Sharon Nobilio, Donna Hartley, Nicole Caple, and Sharon Monrean read and reread versions of sometimes the same chapters and patiently offered help and suggestions for improvement.

I learned much about writing chapters from author Gloria Kempton, whom I met through a Writers Digest University course.

Leila Kheiry, news director at KRBD, helped me fashion a cogent narrative. My writing companion, Ketchikan superintendent of schools, Bob Boyle, read the manuscript and provided invaluable help, as did Biz Robbins, Terry Pyles, and Dave Rubin.

Researching the book brought me back in touch with Doug Hostetter, now director of the United Nations Office of the Mennonite Central Committee. Fifty years ago, I met Doug in Tam Ky performing alternative service with Viet Nam Christian Service. Our views of the US involvement in Vietnam were polar opposites, but we found common ground at the Quang Tin Province Prison where we both worked to improve the stark living conditions endured by the men, women, and children incarcerated there. Doug contributed the photo in chapter 11.

Finally, but not least, I want to thank my wife, Elaine, for her patience and especially for proofing the manuscript and our daughters, Elizabeth and Sarah, for their support and encouragement.

APPENDIX

Thai Irritation on Refugees Grows

By HENRY KAMM
Special to The New York Times

SONGKHLA, Thailand, Jan. 23—Mistreatment of Vietnamese refugees seeking asylum in southern Thailand is mounting at an alarming rate, in a climate dominated by growing resentment at the continuing arrival of their small fishing boats.

The Thai Government is annoyed that the rest of the world, particularly the United States is not taking Indochinese refugees out of Thailand at a rate faster than that at which they arrive and enter the camps here. In this atmosphere, and in contravention of assurances by Prime Minister Kriangsak Chamanand, officials in the southern provinces mistreat the new refugees, all "boat people" from Vietnam, with impunity.

According to witnesses, the officials refuse to allow some boats to land, forcibly push boats and their passengers out to sea in this season of monsoon storms, jail other refugees for "illegal entry" and plunder their meager belongings. Multiple rape and other personal abuses have taken place, the witnesses say.

Food, although paid for by the United Nations High Commissioner for Refugees, is reportedly often denied in the seaside camp here, where 603 refugees await a chance to go to another country.

Refusal to let boats land is regarded as the most widespread denial of humane treatment and traditional custom. They are being turned away even though most of the craft that get this far are no longer seaworthy, supplies of water, food and fuel are exhausted and most passengers are more dead than alive from exposure, seasickness, deprivation of food and water and extreme fatigue. Children make up roughly one third of the refugee total.

On Dec. 28, Prime Minsister Kriangsak said in an interview with The New York Times that Thai policy, based on Buddhist principles, did not allow denial of the right to land. He reiterated this in a conversation with leading State Department officials, including Patricia M. Derian, Assitant Secretary for Human Rights, last Monday.

The preceding day, Robert B. Oakley, Deputy Assistant Secretary of State for East Asian and Pacific Affairs, discussed the Thai policy with the provincial governor and vice governor here. But on the same day that the Prime Minister was meeting with the Americans, a boat carrying 34 refugees sought time to repair its engine but was ordered by local authorities at gunpoint to leave for the open sea within 10 minutes.

The action was averted by the presence here of Michael Harpold, special assistant to the director of the United States Immigration and Naturalization Service. On his own authority he guaranteed that the United States would accept the refugees, and they were allowed ashore.

Mr. Harpold was here to gather material for testimony that Leonel J. Castillo, the director, is expected to present before a House subcommittee this week, in a hearing on allowing 7,000 more "boat people" into the United States.

Made in the USA
Middletown, DE
04 November 2023